DYING TO DIVORCE

PART I: OMAHA

RICHARD SCHATZ
with
KRISTINE M

DYING TO DIVORCE
PART I: OMAHA

©2016 Richard Schatz with Kristine Marsh.

All rights reserved.

Printed in the United States of America

Book design and layout by Barbara Lindenberg, Bluebird Designs.
Front cover design by Douglas Marsh.

ISBN: 978-0-692-78525-6

Dying to Divorce Publications

The events as portrayed in *Dying To Divorce* are true. They are based on facts contained in Richard Schatz' client case files. Names, characters, businesses, places, events and incidents are either the products of the authors' imagination or used in a fictitious manner. Any resemblance to actual persons, living or dead, or actual events is purely coincidental.

PREFACE

Richard Schatz, forensic financial specialist, originally practiced in California and Nevada and now lives in Houston. Kristine Marsh, MBA, owns and operates her own Educational Technology company in Bradenton,Florida. They came together not only from opposite ends of the United States, but with totally unrelated business backgrounds, skills and education. Together they collaborated on the writing of this book.

True events from Richard's client case files, combined with Kristine's creative expressions of prose and sentence structure, resulted in what you will be reading in this book, entitled *Dying to Divorce: Part I-Omaha.*

The co-authors put together a team of participants, who are listed under Acknowledgments, and who provided valuable assistance in the development of the social and family backgrounds of the people depicted in this book.

PART 1: OMAHA

ACKNOWLEDGMENTS

We wish to acknowledge those who provided valuable historical and creative assistance during the course of our writing *Dying to Divorce: Part I-Omaha.*

They are:

- Kathie McStravick, who introduced Kristine Marsh to Richard Schatz

- Douglas Marsh, Florida graphic artist, who designed the front cover of this book

- Barbara Hurst, for her outstanding editorial skills

- Deborah Blonstein, Dallas copywriter, for her creative character names

- Barbara Lindenberg, for her editing and final preparation of the manuscript

PART 1: OMAHA

PROLOGUE

It is a gorgeous sunny day with clear skies and warm breezes in Nassau. Russell Jenkins and his assistant Jean Cameron are thrilled to be working in Nassau, away from their desks in Omaha, Nebraska. Breakfast on the patio overlooking the ocean is just what they need to get motivated for their big client meeting this morning.

Russell is a self-made man climbing the professional and social ladders with his beautiful wife Melodie by his side. Things have not been great recently. He feels enormous pressure to keep up with his well-heeled in-laws, his socially active wife, and four kids who require a lot of time and money to keep them happy. The well-being of his family and his position within his company might depend on the outcome of this early morning meeting.

Back in Omaha, Zach Willis is helping his wife Beth get their two young daughters off to school. He treasures these mornings with just the four of them at home. Sometimes the girls bicker, but not today. It is peaceful and quiet in their kitchen. This won't last long. On his way to the office downtown, he drops the girls at their school. Zach is a homicide detective with the Omaha Police Department.

His day is about to change.

Chapter One

Russ glanced at his Tag Heuer again. It was 9 a.m. here in the Bahamas and 8 a.m. back home in Omaha. Russel Jenkins was a very handsome man at forty-eight years old. He was almost six-and-a-half feet tall with just enough silver speckled throughout his thick and plentiful charcoal hair to give him the look of a very wise and distinguished man. He had maintained his masculine physique from his younger years of working out seven days a week. Whatever he did, he did well or he didn't do it at all. As Challenge Life's Vice President for Omaha's twenty regional offices, a husband, and father of four, he did not have the time to work out as much as he would like to, but still managed to hit the gym, or a trail, five days every week, even when traveling.

He extended his left arm to untuck his watch from his Armani black suit jacket again. 9:15. He felt anxious today. He and his Traveling

Executive Assistant, Jean, were waiting to meet with a potential new client, who was fifteen minutes late so far. This client would bring a net worth of over twenty-two million; big business for his company. Too big, he thought, to send anyone else from the office to reel this one in. In fact, so big that Russ was keeping this one to himself, waiting to close the business himself before disclosing the potential to avoid over-enthusiasm among his corporate office.

9:24 a.m. His phone rang. "Mr. Jenkins! Mr. Jenkins! It's Melodie", Glaucia, their long time housekeeper, sobbed uncontrollably. "Melodie has been shot! I called 911 and they are on their way. Come home. Come home, now!"

Russ arranged to have a company jet ready for him and Jean immediately and he arrived at his home near 196th Street at roughly noon. He had a great deal of pride in his home. He'd worked hard for it. Spanning over 4,500 square feet, his stone and brick sprawling house had precision lush landscaping with a sea of colors including tulips, roses and Melodie's favorite, white daisies. The double door entrance to the home was magnificent with impressive pillars extending up to an upstairs guest apartment and balcony. Yet, it was also cozy with a romantic, beautifully hand-crafted wooden swing so Melodie and Russ could take in the sights and smells of their gorgeous flowers. Well, typically it was just Melodie enjoying the swing since Russ was traveling two or three weeks per month.

Their four children took full advantage of the spacious property, inside and out. With three girls and one boy, ranging in age from 11 to 20, they definitely needed their space.

He arrived to a horrific and chaotic scene. Countless police vehicles were scattered throughout the perimeter of his property; yellow crime tape tightly wrung around his trees; a handful of news crews were trying to catch their big break of the story, as dozens of onlookers were waiting for a glimpse of the tragedy that had happened at the Jenkins's home that morning. Russ suddenly felt an unbearable twisting sensation in his stomach as he saw the white coroner's van backed up onto the driveway. As he slowly came to a stop near his home, inside his Mercedes Benz CLK, it was silent. It was surreal. Only the beauty of classical music pumping from his Sirius radio, featuring a rich cello solo, in the luxury of white leather and wood grained trim was heard; yet only the sights of tragedy were seen outside. As he took in a deep breath to gain the courage to approach the chaos, he slowly opened his car door. The news vultures were immediately flocking to him. "Mr. Jenkins, do you know who did this to your wife?" "Mr. Jenkins, where were you at the time she was shot?" The questions continued and he was unable to utter any type of response.

"Are you Mr. Jenkins?" asked a police officer. A homicide detective, to be exact.

"I need to see my wife" Russ whispered. "I need to see my wife! Where is my wife?" Russ was now pushing his way through to try to make his way into his home, but was stopped by four police officers. They were gentle but firm.

"Mr. Jenkins, I am sorry. This is a crime scene under investigation. You cannot go inside."

"Mr. Jenkins, I am Zachary Willis, the chief homicide detective for the Omaha Police Department assigned to this case. May we have a few words? Is Melodie Jenkins your wife?"

"Yes. Yes, Detective. Melodie is my wife" Russ managed to mutter.

He'll never forget how his breath was taken away from the first sight of her, twenty-eight years ago, sipping her morning cup of caffeine while studying at the Java Jay, on Creighton Campus. She was stunning. Her strikingly long, beautiful red hair flowing over her slender shoulders brought out her gorgeous green eyes. Her long smooth legs were daintily crossed at the ankles. He was in such awe of her beauty that he did not notice her firm warning to him the first time around. She repeated, "Hey, if you want to live to see tomorrow, you better put out that cigarette!"

Nearly tripping over his own two feet, Russ quickly returned to the entrance, flicked the cigarette out and reentered the Java Jay. They made brief eye contact and she whispered a 'thank you', and he replied with "I don't really smoke anyway". He quickly ordered his double tall bold coffee, black, and got on his way to class. That's it? That's all I could say? Why didn't I talk to her more? Get her name? What's her major? He continued to question himself since being short of words was certainly not typical for him, especially around women. He'd hoped to run into her again, but then again, he knew he had no time for a relationship. Relationships just 'mess with success'; that was his motto anyway. That's why he was careful to keep women at a distance. Just for fun, when time permitted and when the need was calling.

Russ just made it to his ECO 203 class on time, slipping into his seat right at 7:45 a.m. With only eighteen students in his class, his on-time arrival, which is deemed as late at Creighton, did not go unnoticed.

"Mr. Jenkins, you are late!" Professor Riley barked. "If you had a one-shot opportunity to convince the Board of Directors of Butterfield

& Son in Bermuda to fund your project, you just lost it!" he scolded.

"You are right, Professor Riley. It won't happen again." Russ assured him.

Creighton University is rated as the #1 private college in the midwest. They achieved that high ranking by having high standards for their Catholic student body along with an unprecedented number of club opportunities. Not to mention their standing in the NCAA. Built in 1878, it sat on over 4,000 acres in Omaha and maintained much of its beautiful original architectural charm.

"Okay, let's get back to pricing strategies. You should have read the chapter regarding price elasticity in a micro environment, and completed the Case Study for your product in your..." Professor Riley continued. Russ's attention was on the beauty he had just met at the Java Jay. She was gorgeous, confident and feisty. A woman like that would make quite a memorable night! He decided he'd have to visit the Java Jay again in hopes to having a second chance of making a memorable impression on her.

Russ was in his fourth year of schooling at Creighton with only one year left before graduating with his MBA, with an emphasis in Finance. His GPA was an impressive 5.0. He didn't make it this far this successfully by allowing himself to be distracted by the social conventions of partying and Greek life. Instead, he took a heavy class load, year round, completing extra assignments when given the opportunity. And, he certainly didn't allow women to distract him from his studies. He had women, though. Plenty of women. Just one night stands and some 'girlfriends' with no strings attached.

He was smart about it, though. He always used protection. Well, with the exception of Isabella. He met Isabella in the sauna at Kiewit Fitness

Center his freshman year. Russ was exhausted after another strenuous workout. He'd lifted weights for forty-five minutes. It was 'upper day', so he focused on bi's, tri's and back, and then he ran the track for an hour. The next day he would repeat the process, but focus on legs. This was his daily routine. He hit the sauna to relax his muscles, simply draping a towel over himself. The heat took his breath away for a moment as he closed his eyes and took in a deep inhale, smelling the distinct scent of hot cedar.

"May I join you?" He heard the sound of a delicate voice.

"Sure. Wait! What are you doing in here? How'd you get in here?", Russ replied in a whisper, but with surprise being that the saunas at Kiewit definitely were not co-ed.

She was stunning with gracefully long brunette hair, pulled into a ponytail, tickling the middle of her back, just below the tie on her bikini top. Her body tone told him that she must have a similar workout routine as he did, but he'd never seen her there.

"Well," the sweet voice started to explain, "the sauna in the ladies' locker room was out of order, so I thought I'd sneak over to the guys'. Is that okay?"

"Y-yes, of course. Hi, I'm Russ. I haven't seen you here before. When do you usually come to Kiewit?" he asked, trying not to sound too eager.

"I'm actually a visitor. My cousin is a student here and she gave me a pass so I could work out while she's at work. This place is amazing! I've never seen a college gym quite like this place."

"Right", Russ agreed. "If Creighton sets out to do something, they do it like no other! So, do you have a name?" he teased.

"Ah, yes!" she giggled. "I'm Isabella".

The two continued to exchange pleasantries…where she's from, what she does, what's his major, when he plans to graduate. He can't remember how pleasantries turned into romance, but he definitely remembers her sliding her hand beneath his towel and before he knew it, they were making love right there in the sauna. The heat of the sauna, the spontaneity, and the risk of getting caught added to the intensity. And just like that, she was gone.

The experience was erotic! He'd never forgotten it and he certainly did not regret it. But, he was a nervous wreck for months afterwards, not having used protection. He'd never really stopped worrying about her showing up at his door with some kid, claiming it's his; and it took months for him to stop worrying about the possibility of him contracting something from her. So now Russ 'packs' no matter where he is, ever. He'd always wondered whatever became of Isabella.

Chapter Two

The sound of his roommate's alarm was jolting—every single morning. It was probably even jolting for the three co-eds who lived upstairs. Although the Capitol Rows apartment complex was off-campus, all but two renters were Creighton students. The apartment building was modern with a spacious lobby area with a great deal of seating for students to congregate, including a few tables students use as desks for group projects and a big screen TV for football parties. Darren and Russ did not know each other prior to moving in together. Capitol Rows had a list of roommate seekers posted and that's how they found one another. Their apartment was of ample size, just over one thousand square feet. They each had their own bedroom and bathroom with a common living area and open kitchen. Since Darren's parents were footing the bill for all of Darren's college expenses, and he even talked them into paying a bit more for the apartment, Darren got the en suite bedroom. Russ loved it there. Besides the laundry area being a community room, and Darren's alarm clock, it was perfect.

Why he needed the alarm so damn loud, Russ would never know! Of course, maybe since he stayed out partying several nights per week, coming home in a drunken stupor and therefore unable to wake up from the simple rising of the sun, might have something to do with it. However, that damn alarm was set to its highest volume and took at least a minute before it actually awakened Darren. Russ actually planned his morning accordingly to avoid the whole thing. He woke up without an alarm by 5:00 a.m. After a quick thirty-minute run, he reviewed his school work from the night before, making sure everything was fresh in his mind and that he hadn't missed anything in his assignments. If time permitted, he read the next chapter, or he would write a persuasive argument about a current event to entice his professors to give him extra points in the grade book, or simply to accumulate 'brownie points' in the Russ-bank, which came in handy from time to time if he didn't ace a test. After a quick shower, he'd be out the door, before that blasted alarm started to ring.

He's been leaving a little earlier lately to improve his odds of running into the beauty at the Java Jay again. He was not one to need coffee; that's what his morning runs were for. But, since seeing her earlier in the week, he'd returned to the Java Jay daily. The first few days he went back at the same time he ran into her the first time. Since that hadn't worked, he was mixing up his schedule. That day, it was only 7:05 a.m.

"Good morning again. What can I get you this morning?" asked the bubbly blonde barista behind the counter. By now you would think she would know what Russ got in the morning, however, he ordered something different every time to keep things interesting.

Russ smiled at her. She was probably a student here and working her way through college. He respected that; unlike his roommate whose parents paid for everything, thus having no appreciation for the opportunities he'd been given. He certainly had no respect for Russ and his rigorous schedule.

"What would you say is the healthiest morning drink on your menu?" he asked.

"That's an odd question coming from a guy who smokes!" barked a familiar voice. He quickly looked to his right and there she was!

"I don't believe I caught your name the first time we met. I'm Melodie."

"Well, hello Melodie. What a nice surprise to run into you again. I'm Russ" he replied and quickly responded to the barista to just surprise him with some kind of smoothie laced with extra protein.

"And, I really don't smoke!" he assured Melodie with a gentle laugh.

"Uh huh" she replied with a half-smile.

Russ asked the barista to make whatever drink Melodie would like and offered to put it on his JayBucks$ card.

"Does this count as a date?" she asked, to which Russ responded, "only if you sit down and drink it with me".

After several minutes of chatting about their experiences at Creighton, Russ found himself unable to take his eyes off of hers. Those strikingly green eyes captured him, pulling him into her soul. Something about her was different. He couldn't focus on all the words she was saying, but the sound of her voice was intoxicating. She wasn't like most of the other women he dated; she was simple and pure yet she seemed driven like him.

Russ looked down at his watch. "Ah, crap! I'm sorry, I have to run! If I'm late for my Econ. class again, Riley will have it in for me! How about meeting me this afternoon at one o'clock outside the St. John's Parish?"

"Maybe" Melodie hesitated. "I have much to do but I will try." That was partly true and partly a lie. She always had much to do, however, she also wasn't eager to get involved with any kind of relationship. Who had time? And the drama they often lead to! She surely didn't want to get into a situation where one of them wanted more than the other. Those were so hard to get out of! But, something about Russ really grabbed her. He was confident yet he didn't come across as arrogant; and he was gorgeous!

Chapter Three

Russ pleaded with Detective Willis. "Where is my wife? What happened to my wife?"

"Mr. Jenkins, I am terribly sorry but your wife has been shot. It pains me to inform you that she did not make it." This was Zachary's eighteenth year as a homicide detective and this was the forty-third time he'd had to notify someone of the death of a loved one. It never got easier! Never! He had to find a way to allow his heart to grow cold during the investigation because it was just too emotionally draining and he cannot bring his work home with him. However, notifying a family member would never get easier and there is no way to grow cold to that.

Russ fell to his knees sobbing. His hands cupped his face as he rocked in agony.

"No. No. No. No. That can't be. I want to see her! I need to see her!

I need to hold her!" The pain he felt in his heart could be heard and felt by Zachary and the handful of remaining police officers and detectives still on the premises, not to mention the news media.

"Mr. Jenkins, I know this is a very difficult time" Detective Willis said, as he gently reached down to help him back up to his feet. "I am here to bring your wife's killer to justice, so I must ask you questions now to give us the best chance of catching this guy. Let's move to the bench so you can get off your feet."

As they walked a few steps to the bench, the detective continued to take notes and began his questions. "Do you know of anyone who would want to hurt her, Mr. Jenkins? Is it possible Melodie would take her own life? When did you last see her? How long has Glaucia worked for you? What was her relationship with Melodie like?"

Russ couldn't think of anyone who would want to hurt Melodie; she certainly wouldn't take her own life; he just saw her that morning before he left for the Bahamas; and Glaucia adored her.

A tight knot twisted in Russ's stomach as he asked the detective, "Oh Lord, my children. Have they been notified?"

"As far as I know, Mr. Jenkins, they have not been notified. To your recollection, were they home this morning?"

"No. They wanted to spend the night at their grandparents' last night so we took them there after dinner. I need to go pick them up before they get on the bus to come home. I don't want them arriving to this scene." Russ didn't know how he would break this terrible news to his kids. Especially RJ and Elizabeth. Melodie had been the one 'constant' in RJ's life as he learned to cope with, and adjust to life with autism. Elizabeth, the baby of the family, and Melodie were the closest of all of them.

"I know you're tired and devastated, Mr. Jenkins? Here's my card. Please call me in the morning after you get some rest and we'll pick up from here," Zachary requested. "And, please, stay in town to help us catch this guy. You don't have any other travel plans, do you?"

Russ quietly responded, assuring the detective that he would take the kids back to their grandparents' for a few days and that he'd cancel all his trips until they caught this bastard.

"Very well, Mr. Jenkins. I will see you tomorrow."

Zachary returned to his black Honda Accord. The car wasn't fancy but it was dependable and nice enough, with dark tinted windows—as dark as the law permits. It also gave him the privacy he needed as a detective.

"Joe, Zach here. Jenkins will be leaving his property in the next few minutes. His white Mercedes is parked on the south side of 196th so he'll most likely be headed east. He says he's going to pick up his kids from school and then to their grandparents' place. Keep a tail on him. His plate reads JENKS10M. Report back to me where he goes and what he does."

Joe had been on the police force for only one year. Although he was young, he was smart, and wiser than his twenty-six years and he loved the chase. He'd always been a bit socially awkward since he grew up with a speech impediment and severe acne. He'd tried to make friends, and would have been a dedicated friend for anyone to have, but the other kids wouldn't give him a chance. So, rather than spending his time at high school parties and socializing with the girls, he'd spent his time reading crime stories, and solving neighborhood crimes on his own. If the neighborhood gossip revealed a simple tree TP-ing, he'd take it upon himself to wait in watch of possible suspects. He'd use his keen hearing to eavesdrop in the school locker room and lunch room, until he was able to out the bad guys. He loved it. And he was good at it. Now on the police force, Joe made the best possible undercover cop in the area. Needless to say, as with many adolescent boys, he had grown up to be a handsome man, but was forever trained as socially awkward.

Joe recognized the emblem of a Mercedes approaching from his review mirror. Yes, this was Jenkins. License plate matched. He knew what the plate meant. "Arrogant bastard", he thought. This pompous ass won't ever amount to the ten million he aspires to be! Joe slowly pulled out to follow Russ after Russ made a quarter turn and he followed a safe distance behind.

After traveling less than eight miles, Russ pulled into a hotel and checked in. "Zach, yeah, your man just checked into a Hilton Garden Inn on Chicago Street."

"How long did it take him to get checked in?" Zachary asked.

"Less than a minute. He walked up to the front counter and the woman behind the counter handed him his key. He must've made reservations on the way over." Joe responded. "I took time-stamped pictures for you."

Zach first made a stop to grab a double bacon cheeseburger with ketchup, mayo, pickle and onion only, a large fry with no salt, and a gigantic Diet Coke and then pulled into the Hilton Garden Inn parking lot a few spaces over from Russ's car and waited in watch. After only one hour, Russ was on the move again.

Chapter Four

Russ was sure to get to the Parish a few minutes before 1:00 p.m. in hopes that Melodie would be able, or willing, to meet him there as proposed earlier at the Java Jay. Again, he couldn't get her beautiful green eyes and red hair out of his mind all day. His daydreams wandered to places far too far, far too soon. He imagined her wearing a sexy blue dress with wide but loose straps, and him leaning down to place his mouth onto her thin but tender lips. He kissed her gently, while his hand slipped the loose strap off her shoulder. He imagined her beautiful flawless skin, and him tracing her neck and shoulder line with his fingertips, giving her goose bumps. His hand graced down the low V-neck of her dress and he felt the outline of her full breasts…

"Hey Casanova! I made it!" she teased as she approached him, in her comfortable jeans and baggy shirt. She'd hoped she'd have time to get back to her apartment to change into something a bit more flattering before she met him, but her day had been just too busy. But, she also wanted to be herself and she was comfortable in comfortable clothes!

Russ laughed, "Casanova, huh? Who says?"

"You know I'm far too busy to take an afternoon hiatus, but somehow you seduced me at the coffee shop this morning and here I am!"

"Well, thank you for taking a few minutes out of your very busy day to see me. I love the Parish. No matter how many times a week I'm here, I still am overwhelmed with the art, architecture and history of this place." Russ said softly as he and Melodie took a moment to take in the sight.

The St. John's Parish truly was breathtaking. Outside, the chapel was carefully crafted with tan brick with two steeples raised to the heavens. Each steeple had a cross atop. The main entrance was magnificent with a huge mahogany door beneath a gorgeous brick arc. Above the door were stained glass windows climbing up the front of the facade, leading to another large cross.

Upon entry into the chapel, worshipers were greeted with a series of white pillars spanning from the back of the chapel to the altar. Each pillar blossomed with gold trim traveling up and over the one-hundred-twenty-five-foot majestic ceiling. The gold had been a result of donated jewelry, watches and medals from students as well as Mrs. Edward Creighton herself. Stained glass windows lined the entire chapel, with windows illuminating the chapel with a beautiful blue hue, spilling in from the heavens.

Russ and Melodie slowly walked around the inside of the parish, pointing to different characteristics of the stained glass, wood work, or décor that 'spoke to them' personally. Melodie found herself to be a bit fidgety, not knowing what to do with her hands because what she really wanted to do was to grab this gorgeous man by the waist and pull him into her and kiss him! But it was far too soon for such behavior and it surely was not the right place. She felt her heart beating a few extra beats faster, she felt flushed and the girlish side of her came through, which hadn't been out in a long time. She was typically all business. Serious. She couldn't deny that there was something about Russ that captivated her, beyond his good looks. They definitely had chemistry. Russ would find an excuse every now and then to touch Melodie, to either get her attention to point something out, or to maneuver past her, gently placing his hand on her hips as he slipped by her. Russ was pleased that she seemed responsive to his subtle touching and did not pull back. In fact, he was getting the vibe that she was in to him, too.

After about an hour, it was time for them to get back to reality. They both had heavy study loads and busy schedules. But Russ assured Melodie that he would be free that night around 7:30 if she'd like to come over for dinner or a drink. He wanted to fulfill the daydream he'd had about her all day! She gently declined but assured him that she would give him a call sometime.

She did call him a few days later, and things progressed rather quickly between the two of them over the next six weeks. They found ways to squeeze in morning coffee, lunches, and nice wine several times a week. However, Melodie did her best to avoid being at his place, or him at hers, for dinner because she was afraid she'd end up getting into a physical relationship. She tried her best to live her life in a Godly manner and the temptation was very strong towards Russ. Russ began to find this very frustrating. He had always found it easy to woo women and it usually took no time for things to heat up in the bedroom. Melodie was different though. As frustrating as it was, it was even more refreshing. She would make a very good, honorable wife for someone someday. But for now, he was ready for some good no-strings-attached sex. If it wasn't going to be with Melodie, he knew just who to call. He really liked Melodie and she would definitely be upset if he hooked up with someone else. But they didn't have a committed relationship yet. Right? Right he convinced himself.

"Hey sexy, what are you doing tonight?"

"I'm working until 6, what about you?"

"Do you want to come over for a drink?"

"Yes, see you at your place at 6:30ish. Can't wait. I've missed you. I have a new fun idea for us tonight".

What was it about her that was so intoxicating to him? Okay, that's what was intriguing about her. Damn, she got him going! She was sexually expressive and not afraid to show it. They had met at a party that Russ's roommate threw a couple of years ago. He wasn't thrilled about the party because he'd had a paper due the next day but his roommate insisted on celebrating some unimportant event and inviting over a bunch of people. Russ was social for a little bit, but then went to his room, put his headphones on to drown out the noise and had got to work on his paper. About forty-five minutes later, in came this adorable slightly drunk, flirtatious girl asking why he was being unsocial. She was wearing a short but flowy black skirt with high heels and a bedazzled belt draping her hips. Her white button-down fitted shirt was unbuttoned just low enough so that her full breasts were sure to tantalize. She had long jet-black hair and milky white skin.

"Oh, hey. I have a paper due tomorrow so I'm just working on that. Aren't you having fun out there?" Russ asked the promiscuous girl.

"Aww. That's no fun for you! Yea, the party is good, but now I'm interested in what is going on in here. What's your paper on?" she pretended to be interested.

"It's a business case analysis ultimately comparing the net present values of two business options. The two options are..." Mid-sentence, she draped her left leg over him and sat on his lap, straddling him, with her arms thrown around his neck and her beautiful, inviting cleavage right up against him.

"That definitely doesn't sound like fun" she said in a playful tone.

"No, no. You're right it's not" he eagerly agreed. "It's not at all. Do you have some something better in mind?" And with that, she reached down and felt that he was already getting aroused.

"I think I'd like to get to know Darren's roommate a little better. I've heard so much about him, you know," she whispered as she bit her lower lip.

As he responded in agreement, he leaned in to kiss her neck while tracing his fingers from her delicate neck, down to her lush breasts as he began unbuttoning the rest of the remaining buttons. She made a quick twist to the fastener on his jeans and sprang it open with ease, and carefully unzipped him while they continued to kiss passionately. Russ reached into his top desk drawer to grab a condom while she lifted up his T-shirt to reveal his cut, shaved chest. She sat back for a moment just to take in this gorgeous sight, as she felt the muscles on his chest and ran her fingers all the way down to feel just how ready he was for her. He slid his jeans down just enough and together, they rolled the condom down into position. Without ever leaving his chair, she lowered herself down onto him and together they let out a deep heavy sigh. God, he needed this break!

They had chemistry as if they'd made love many times before; they naturally moved together just right. It didn't take long before they both reached climax-her first, then him. He could have much sooner, but he was waiting for her, which required incredible restraint. They smiled, then laughed at how bad, yet good they were. Russ tapped her gently to get up so he could clean up real quick at which time, he noticed he hadn't even locked the door! Just imagine if someone from the party came in looking for her! So, they laughed some more, and she laid down on his bed to recuperate, which Russ thought was a great idea. They laid together, she resting her head on that massive chest of his, and their hearts still beating like crazy. Russ figured this would wrap up the night and he wouldn't get back to his paper, so he reached over to set his alarm for the early morning, just in case. He never did ask her name.

He didn't wake again until morning and his friend had already left but she left a sticky note on his computer:

Sorry I distracted you from your paper!

Wow, what an amazing night. Call me sometime, Jean

402-555-1212

The night was amazing! The sex was the best he'd ever had! She was vivacious, confident and very responsive. He'd definitely hang on to her number. And, now he knew her name.

Since then, Jean and Russ had a great friendship. They grew to really care about each other, but never had a committed relationship, and the sex continued to be out of this world. And without drama. She had other boyfriends and Russ continued to play the field, but they were always drawn back to one another. They were like the 'one constant' in each other's lives.

Russ made sure the apartment was clean and ready for Jean. He knew she liked Riesling wine and he had a nice bottle chilled for her. He'd already called Melodie to let her know that he was busy studying for the night and that he'd talk with her tomorrow.

At 6:33 p.m. there was a soft knock on the door. Russ quickly rushed to the door, excited to see her. It had been a few months since he'd had some time with Jean. She looked beautiful as ever, in her work clothes. She wore a low-cost, knock-off designer pants suit with high heels to help compensate for her short 5'3" stature. Her signature low-cut shirt under her suit jacket made her look professional yet sexy at the same time. If anyone could pull off a suit like that, it was Jean. Her long black hair was pulled back into a pony tail and she had a smile that melted Russ's heart. Jean was an intern at a small financial company. She was an assistant to the Executive Assistant, doing data entry, filing and research. She felt like she could do more, but she had to take what she could as an intern.

Russ handed her the perfectly chilled glass of Riesling. "So tell me, you provocative woman," Russ inquired, "what new idea do you have in mind for us tonight?"

She had a gift bag dangling from her arm, but she teased, "easy does it, Stallion. You'll see. I've missed you! Let's sip some wine and catch up a bit first".

'Catch up' to her always meant foreplay. Small talk with gentle touching, a little kissing, maybe a foot rub. It really was nice, but Russ was anxious to get to the point. But, he was patient. She finally revealed the secret inside the goodie bag. It was some kind of vibrating cock ring. So they tried it. It was loud, annoying and uncomfortable, so after a few attempts, thinking they were just using it wrong, it got flung to the floor and they made love the tried and true way. She got an 'A' for effort, though; he loved that she wasn't afraid to try new things.

He didn't tell her about Melodie. Although the sex and physical connection with Jean was out of this world, he just felt like there was something deeper with Melodie. So, he never told Jean about Melodie and he never told Melodie about Jean, with whom he'd now had a sexual relationship for the past two years. He never would have believed back then that their one year sexual affair would have lasted a lifetime. And, he sure as hell never would have imagined that she would still be the 'one constant' in his life during such a traumatic time as this.

Chapter Five

Russ first pulled up to Kelsey Grammar School to retrieve Beth from school. At the front office, he simply stated that he was there to get Elizabeth. From the tone of his voice, the school secretary asked, "Is everything okay, Mr. Jenkins?" He responded simply by stating, "I'm here for Beth. Please send for her immediately."

Just a few minutes later, he watched his daughter practically skip down the hall, happy to get out of school early. It was not terribly uncommon, as her parents would surprise them with little family getaways every now and then. Her smile was a ray of sunshine. Beaming. How was he going to tell her about her mother? Beth was the youngest of the four children at eleven years old. As the baby of the family, she was the closest to her mother. Melodie insisted on naming her after her own mother, knowing this fourth child would be their last. She was top of her class in academics and had a unique athletic prowess about her. She played sports year round: volleyball, basketball and softball.

"Hi Daddy!" she squealed with a hug. "I thought you were in the Bahamas for a few days."

Russ forced a smile and simply let her know that his trip was postponed and that she would get to go with him to pick up Kimberly and Ashley, too.

Next stop was Washington Middle School. He called ahead to the school this time, so Kimberly was waiting inside the office for him when he arrived. She was not your typical thirteen-year-old girl. She shared a common trait with RJ, but her autism was not as severe. She did fairly well in school academically, but not as well as her sisters. She did inherit the athletic gene, though, so she was quite active and very fit. She was very sweet and likeable and made friends fairly easily, although she always felt a bit socially awkward.

"Hey, Dad. What's up? Why do I get to leave school early today?" she asked eagerly. "I'm not complaining. I hate school. So I'm so glad to leave, but what's up? I'm not in trouble am I?"

"No, sweetheart. God, no. You are not in trouble. Beth is waiting for us in the car. I'll explain later." he reassured her. "Besides, you're doing quite well in school! I'm proud of you! You should start enjoying it!" he encouraged.

Ashley was the oldest girl. She took after both of her parents. She was stunning. Tall. Gorgeous thick red hair, athletic yet slender build. It was very difficult to keep the boys at bay. She was eager to date boys, but thank goodness, she didn't have her license yet, so she could only go on dates if her parents could drive her. She was forbidden from going in a car with a boy who had his license.

Ashley was not only gorgeous, but she was brilliant. She excelled in everything she did: academics and sports. Like Beth, she was also involved in volleyball and basketball. Unlike her sister, she opted for soccer.

Russ pulled up to Southside High School to get Ashley, where she was a sophomore. She was more suspicious than the other two.

"Dad, what's going on? I thought you went to the Bahamas this morning. Why are you taking me out of school early? I have practice after school and can't miss it. And, I'm missing my AP Math class. I have a test on Monday!" she argued.

Ashley saw Beth and Kimberly in the car. "Dad? What's going on?"

"Girls, we are going to your grandparents. We need some family time. Grandpa is picking up RJ and will meet us there soon." RJ is the oldest of the four children. He was named after Russ and carried his name of Russell Jenkins, Jr. They found that having two Russes under the same roof was quite confusing so it didn't take long before Russ Jr. acquired the nickname 'RJ'. He was autistic. While he learned to manage relationships with friends, family and society at large, it was a struggle and he always needed special schooling and mental health professionals. Melodie was his rock. He was now twenty and managed to graduate from his special school, largely attributed to his mother's support. He was just considering college.

The fifteen-minute drive up I-75 to 480 to Dodge Street to Fairacres, where Melodie's parents lived, seemed like an eternity. Russ kept it light by asking each child about her school day; what they learned and other small talk. But the girls pretty much ignored him anyway, speculating as to why they were pulled from school early. Everything from going to Bahamas with daddy, to the Henry Doorly Zoo and Aquarium (again), to "Dad, where's mom?"

Russ was 'saved by the bell' as they had just pulled up to the majestic driveway of Melodie's parents' home. The stone mailbox displayed a large plaque reading FARNSWORTH. It was an impressive home in one of the most elite Omaha neighborhoods. Charles and Elizabeth Farnsworth were major socialites in the community. Charles managed the Farnsworth family limited partnership which owned twelve high rise office buildings and twenty-thousand acres of ranch property. Elizabeth was a socialite and entertained the wives of Charles' clients and business partners.

Russ didn't bother ringing the bell. Knowing the family was home, he tried turning the knob, but the door was locked, so he simply entered the access code in the key pad and entered the home with his three girls. Charles and RJ were in the kitchen, eating a turkey sandwich prepared by Elizabeth. Elizabeth had left them to enjoy their turkey sandwiches alone while she stepped away for some alone-time in her suite.

Charles and Russ held extended eye contact, as the girls ran to him with hugs. They sensed something was wrong, but Grandpa managed to smile and told them he loved them. After the hugs, Russ and he went to library to talk. Charles could tell that the children did not yet know about their mother and he asked Russ how he'd like to tell them. Russ wanted Charles with him when he told the kids, if he could. And, if Elizabeth could be there, too, he'd appreciate that because the kids were going to need an immense amount of support to hear this unbearable news.

In the meantime, the kids were gathered in the family room, brewing up their own theories about what was going on. Elizabeth was convinced that they were planning a family vacation and it was starting now! Of course, as the youngest and most naïve, that theory was expected.

"I know what's going on." Ashley assured. "This is not good. I think Mom left Dad because he's been running around on her! I never wanted to say anything because I wasn't sure, but that's got to be it! Look, Dad pulled us out of school early; Grandpa is acting weird; and Grandma is in her room because she is so mad at Dad that she can't even look at him!"

"No way, Ashley!" Kimberly refused to believe such an awful thing. "You are wrong! Dad wouldn't do that!"

While Kimberly and Ashley were having their heated debate about whether or not their dad could possibly have an affair on their mom, Russ and Charles returned from the library. They looked tired; exhausted; worried.

"Look, kids, quiet down. Stop arguing." Charles encouraged softly. "We need to talk to you about your mother."

"Dad, she left you didn't she? Didn't she? What did you do? This is your fault!" Ashley yelled at her father. The others sat quietly fighting back tears because whatever it was, they knew it wasn't good, and maybe Ashley was right. So many of their friends' parents were divorced and it was awful for them. Living in separate homes; one parent trying to get the kids to hate the other. It was just awful and now that was going to be their fate too.

"No, Ashley, no. It's not that." Russ assured. Although, how coincidental that what they did not know was that their parents were actually going through a divorce and they had already moved forward with obtaining divorce lawyers. Melodie filed for divorce first, but Russ was expecting it once she uncovered his infidelities, so he was ready. But, no, that's not what was happening today.

"Told ya!" Kimberly smirked at Ashley.

Elizabeth quietly asked her dad, "Dad, where's mom?"

"Kids you know how much your mother and I love you. That will never change. But life is going to change very much for us from this point forward and it won't ever be the same. This morning while I was in the Bahamas, I got a call from the police. They called," he took a deep breath and managed to continue speaking as his voice cracked, "to tell me that someone has hurt your mother".

The kids sat silently, not understanding. Then RJ said, " Dad, let's go see her! Where is she? We will make her better. Let's go!" he encouraged as he stood to get the family out the door.

"RJ, sit down", Russ told him gently. "Your mom is not going to be okay. Very bad people hurt her. Russ began to break down as he told the kids, "your mother is with God now, but she will love you forever and look down on you to protect you forever, with God".

The kids sat silently at first, trying to digest what their father had just said to them. RJ spoke first, "Dad, are you saying that mom is—is— is d-d-ead?"

Charles broke down as well and responded to RJ, "She is safe with God now."

"What the hell happened? Who did this to her? I will kill him! I will kill him! I will kill him!", RJ repeated over and over, as he went into a rage. Russ held RJ tightly, hugging him, until he could calm down. But he was a large man now and with the inability to control his emotions, it was hard. It took every bit of strength and love Russ had to keep him from hurting himself or lashing out and hurting anyone else or anything else around him.

Ashley and Kimberly had broken down into uncontrollable sobs, trying to gasp for breath while holding Russ, screaming, "No! No! No! You're wrong! This can't be! She's okay! No!"

Beth had run to find her grandmother, Elizabeth, who was in her bedroom crying, while holding a picture of Melodie from when she was just a child. Elizabeth embraced young Beth as they both cried uncontrollably. "My dear, your mother loved you more than you know. She will always be with you."

Chapter Six

Melodie thought of her mother as she continued to try to resist the temptation of Russ. She knows her mother would be disappointed in her if she gave in to him, but she was sure Russ could be 'the one'. As much as she tried, her attempts at avoiding late night visits with Russ were fairly short lived. After a couple short months, she invited Russ over for dinner and a movie.

"Hey, Russ" Melodie began, "would you like to come over tonight? I'll make you the best spaghetti you've ever had and we can watch *Dead Poets Society*."

Russ eagerly agreed, but he'd have to finish studying for an important quiz for his Statistics class he had the next day. She assured him that was just fine and convinced him to finish studying at her place while she made dinner. She found him intriguingly sexy when he studied, which was all the time.

This was Russ's style. He far preferred going to his girlfriends' homes than have them come to his place. He always blamed it on his room-mate, Darren, not giving him any privacy, but it was really to avoid his various girlfriends from stopping by when perhaps another girl-friend was over. He had a good feeling about how the night would go. Something told him tonight would be the night they would take their relationship to the next level, although he tried not to get his hopes up knowing where she stood. She made that clear several times. Her voice sounded extra sweet, though. Extra playful. And certainly extra, extra sexy.

Melodie, on the other hand, felt anxious. She couldn't remember the last time she was so nervous about a guy coming over. She wanted everything to be perfect. Of course, he had been to her apartment previously, but just to pick her up to go on a date or to run errands together. He'd never come over just to hang out with her before. She cleaned all day to make sure her place was dusted, vacuumed, and she even scrubbed the bathroom, making sure she got every nook and cranny. She'd catch a glimpse of herself periodically, as she whisked by a mirror. She was 'cleaning clothes' casual. Her gorgeous long red locks danced in her ponytail, and her long legs were draped by a loose-fitting pair of short 'sweats-material' shorts. Her layered light blue sports bra beneath her black racer back tank outlined her curves. She thought she did look pretty sexy, if she may say so herself, but way too casual for a dinner date. So she would definitely have to change. She kind of wanted Russ to see her in her casual garb at some point, though. Being comfortable when you're casual says a lot about a relationship, she thought.

"Crap! Only twenty more minutes!" Melodie said to herself, out loud. She still had to shower and change. There certainly wouldn't be enough time to rewash her hair. She magically turned her ponytail into a bun in one second-flat and hopped into the shower to rinse off as quickly as possible. This time she used her apple blossom body gel. Usually she used fragrance-free which is one of the secrets to her flawless skin. But tonight she wanted to smell daintily beautiful. In only five minutes, she was fresh and clean and even re-shaved her legs. She hopped out of the shower, threw her towel around her to quickly dry off and grabbed her natural lotion to moisturize her legs, arms, hands and belly, moving so quickly there was no way she could get all of the lotion thoroughly rubbed in. He'd be here any minute and she didn't know what to wear yet. She swapped the towel for her thick robe from Restoration Hardware, monogrammed, of course, and 'knock knock knock' on the door!

"Oh my God! You're here already?!" she playfully shouted. "Wait a minute!" She had no choice but to throw on the clothes she had worn all day cleaning, to at least to let him in.

Russ was eager to see what was holding her up. "Hey, sexy. Let me in. You don't have to hide anything!" he responded through the thin apartment door.

When Melodie answered the door, she took his breath away. Her hair was let down from the ponytail, spilling all over her shoulders with the classic 'pony tail bump' still impressed into her hair from being up all day. She was in her loose fitting shorts and racer back tank. She smelled like a beautiful spring day.

"Oh my God, Melodie, you are beautiful." Russ took her by the waist with his right hand and pulled her in to him and gently raised her chin with his left hand. They kissed like they had never kissed before. The passion, the sincerity. He knew he was in love. She let out a single heavy sigh as he kissed her, as if she had been waiting for that moment her whole life. Because she had. She knew at that moment that she was in love with Russ.

"I was just about to change," Melodie explained.

"No, don't. Please don't change, Melodie." Russ pleaded. You are so beautiful just the way you are. I always see you done up for work or class. I want to see you as you are tonight. And here, I'll mess up my hair, too!" Russ teased as he ran his hands every which way through his thick hair.

They both laughed and with some coaxing, Melodie finally agreed not to change. She was so glad she had shaved her legs and slathered lotion all over!

Melodie had cleared a spot for him to study at her desk in her bedroom and she led him to it. She promised to leave him alone while he studied and she would prepare this out-of-the-world spaghetti she couldn't stop talking about, which was apparently a family recipe she had learned from her mother, Elizabeth Farnsworth.

Russ tried to ignore the welcoming queen bed, nicely made up with a simple but elegant ivory comforter with burgundy pillows. In fact, there were too many pillows, taking up half the bed. And sitting among them all was a cute little stuffed fluffy puppy dog with solid black eyes and the cutest little pink tongue.

"Don't give Molly any treats or people food!" she teased.

With that, Melodie went to make her spaghetti. He could tell from the moment he walked in the door that the sauce has been simmering for quite some time. Just how he liked it. And Russ focused on studying for his Statistics quiz. Seriously, when would he really use this stuff anyway? Sure, he wanted to be the leader of a company, but he could hire a statistician! He wouldn't actually be doing the Z-test or T-tests! Nonetheless, Creighton educates for the sake of educating and he'd make sure he earned the top grade.

As Russ read and worked out practice problems, he heard Melodie clinking around, and talking to herself. After about twenty minutes, Melodie entered her room to check in on him to see how his studies were going and he welcomed the interruption. As she went to scurry back out of the room, Russ hollered, "Hey wait! Come back here. You can't come in here and not kiss me before you leave. It's regulation!"

"Regulation, huh? You calling the shots around here now, are you?"

"Uh huh!" he joked as she stole a quick 'regulation kiss'.

The spaghetti was almost as good as she led it up to be! The garlic toast with shredded Italian cheese was delicious, too. And the simple Italian salad with mixed greens, shredded cheese and creamy Italian dressing hit the spot. Of course, the Rutherford Cabernet was the perfect pairing.

Russ tried to help with clean-up, but he clearly didn't quite know the job as Russ got the second bottle of wine opened and got the movie ready. He'd heard *Dead Poets Society* was a great inspiring story. Both Melodie and Russ were into entertainment that improved their brains, rather than amused their brains.

Finally, Russ hit play on the VCR and Melodie curled up next to him on the love-seat. Like her bed, it had way too many pillows, which mostly got tossed to the floor. She explained that her mother helped her furnish her apartment and her mother had particular taste.

With his left arm draped around her waist, she was curled up against his chest. Her right hand was gently tracing his fingers, then along the inside of his thigh. He was wearing Calvin Klein jeans. He really could be a Calvin Klein model. Their eyes met and they began to kiss, passionately. They didn't realize the movie had started. They didn't care. This was the moment they'd both been longing for, although Melodie had been trying to resist, to follow her parents' expectations of her as a lady.

Melodie finally asked Russ with a breathy voice in between short breaks for air, "Russ, should we move to my room? Would you be more comfortable?"

"I'd love that if that's what you want" he managed to reply calmly despite the adrenaline pumping through his body. Melodie already felt him pressing up against her, which excited her far more than she could resist.

"Okay, let's go" she agreed as she took him by the hand, and led him to the bedroom. She set Molly on the nightstand, facing her in the opposite direction, as if the stuffed puppy would actually be exposed to anything traumatic! They both giggled as she slid onto the bed. She helped Russ remove his red RL Polo shirt while she sat on the end of the bed and he stood directly in front of her. She was just mesmerized by the beauty of his chest and arms and abs. Perfect. Everything about him was perfect. She ran her fingers from his forearms up to his muscular shoulders, across his pecs and down his abs. Russ leaned over to kiss her, and gently lifted her whole body at the waist to bring her to the mound of pillows. She looked like an angel amidst the beautiful ivory bedspread and burgundy pillows. There were so many of them surrounding her. She looked like a princess with her long waving red hair spilling from all directions over the pillows, shoulders and over her breasts hidden by her black tank top.

Russ removed Melodie's tank top but left her sports bra on, being careful to allow things to move at her pace. God, she was beautiful. Her full breasts filled the sports bra perfectly, leaving a spectacular cleavage. He ran his hand firmly along her long leg, tracing every muscle and along the bottom of her shorts, right along her panty line. She let out another heavy sign and a faint moan. She wanted this so badly! She wanted him.

"Russ, make love to me tonight."

"Are you sure?"

Melodie assured him she was ready. She struggled with this in her head, but she would just have to make peace with herself later. She could not resist Russ, no matter how much she tried.

The night was magical. The sex was beautiful. Simple. Nothing erotic, but filled with emotion, like he could not explain. Sex with Melodie was different from what it was like with Jean. Both were incredible, but for different reasons. He knew a relationship based on sex never works, which is why he liked to keep it that way, but Melodie was different. Their relationship was based on everything else but sex. He was actually afraid of that very fact.

When Russ told Jean he was going to marry Melodie, she was devastated. Although she never really thought of Russ and her getting married, she simply just never thought of Russ getting married—ever. He was too much of a womanizer. Too much of a player to settle down with one woman. But if he ever were to, she just thought it would be with her. They had chemistry! Opposites attract, she thought! He worked and studied so hard, and she was his release; his fun; his balance. She knew she turned him on like no other, and the love they made was passionate and intense. How could he want to settle down with someone boring like Melodie? Creighton was a small campus. She knew of Melodie from seeing her around campus, but she never saw Russ and Melodie together. She was blindsided by this news.

The Farnsworths were thrilled at the news of the engagement. Their little girl would be twenty-four by the time they got married and her fiancé, twenty-six. He had landed a great sales job at one of the largest life insurance companies in the country, Challenge Life. He had a promising career ahead of him. They knew Russ would be able to provide for their daughter and he treated her like a princess. Charles and Elizabeth gladly began planning the wedding, making sure it would be a night to remember; not only by Russ and Melodie, but also (and perhaps more importantly) by all of their friends. As Omaha socialites, they spared no expense. Taking place at the Hyatt Regency, three hundred guests enjoyed an elegant sit-down dinner, a nine-piece band, personal portraits for all guests, not to mention, monographed sweat shirts for each guest to wear for the reception.

Chapter Seven

Russ thought back to their stunning wedding while showering at the Farnsworth home. Although he was already checked into the Hilton Garden Inn, he stayed at Melodie's parents to remain with his kids and do anything he could to comfort them. But now, it was back to reality and he had to get to the police station. He had promised Detective Willis he would stop by to answer more questions first thing in the morning.

"Mr. Jenkins, thank you for coming in this morning. I can't imagine the hell of a night you had. My family and I prayed for you and your family last night." Zachary said. He noticed Russ looked beat. His eyes were bloodshot and all of his facial muscles just appeared to sag. It was obvious he hadn't slept all night. Who could, after what he'd been through, especially with four kids.

"Thank you, Detective Willis. My family thanks you. I think we are going to need prayers for a very long time. So, how can I help catch this bastard? And please, just call me Russ."

As Russ looked around Zach's office he could see that he was a busy man. Stacks, and stacks, and more stacks, of files were everywhere. How could he function in this disorder, Russ thought? Peeking from behind one of the stacks was what appeared to be a family photograph. He could only see a portion of the picture that revealed Zach on the left and to his right, a blonde woman with only her dirty-blonde hair visible from behind the stacks of files. The picture was taken outside under a tree on a beautiful day. Zach caught Russ's glance at the photo.

He moved the photo fully behind the stack of files to hide it from Russ's view. "I apologize. That was insensitive of me to leave that out under your circumstances, Russ."

"No. No, that's quite alright. Looks like a beautiful family. I would imagine that in your line of work you see so much evil in the world, that it's made you even more protective."

Zach agreed, "You have no idea, Russ. I kiss my wife and two little girls every morning before I leave for work, and kiss them as soon as I get home. I treasure every day, because you never know...." He stops himself. "Well, I know you understand, Russ."

The walls were decorated with cheap store-bought art work, except for a framed quote taken from Sherlock Holmes:

'...when you have eliminated all which is impossible, then whatever remains, however improbable, must be the truth.'
Sherlock Holmes - *The Blanched Soldier*

"So, what can I do for you, Detective?" Russ asked.

"Russ, let's start with the easy stuff. You know most all murder victims are killed by their spouse. I know that's not the case here, but the first thing I have to do, as a formality, is eliminate you as a suspect. So, let's get this out of the way so we can get on with finding the real suspect. Tell me, where were you at the time of your wife's murder?"

Russ scoffed, "Oh my God. You're kidding me!" He quickly realized Zach was not kidding one bit and he calmed down and began answering his questions. "Okay, I got the call from my housekeeper Glaucia that my wife had been shot when I was in the Bahamas on business."

"When did you leave for the Bahamas?"

"At 5:00 a.m. I had a meeting with a client at 9:00 a.m. in the Bahamas. I kissed Melodie good bye as she was sleeping.

She awoke slightly, smiled at me and told me she loves me" Russ tried to explain while his voice began to crack from holding back emotions.

"You told me last night your kids spent the night at Melodie's parents. Why did they spend the night at their grandparents on a school night? Is that a common occurrence?" Zach inquired.

"Fairly common. Every now and then they do. This particular night, Charles, Melodie's father, had rented a movie that Beth, my youngest daughter, wanted to see; so they begged to stay over at their place to watch a movie and have pizza. Melodie and I thought it would also be a good time for us to be able to enjoy a romantic night together at home alone before I left for my trip."

"Did things work out …romantically…for you and Melodie like you'd hoped, Russ?" Zach asked with a slight blush and a sideways smile.

Russ's perfect white smile finally emerged as he proudly answered,

"Well, Detective, you're getting a bit personal now, but if you really must know, yes, it sure did! I thank God I got to make love to my wife before....before..."

"Russ, tell me about your marriage to Melodie. Did you have a happy marriage?"

Russ told Zachary about the first time he saw Melodie at the Java Jay at Creighton 24 years ago; and he told him about the date at the Parish and the moment he knew she was the one, the famous "Spaghetti Dinner Night". He went on to explain their life after marriage in 1990.

Life was good for the newlyweds. Russ was a natural at financial sales. His type-A personality, combined with his great looks, charismatic personality and financial background made his success at Challenge Life soar rapidly. After only two years, he and Melodie were able to build their dream home on 196th where they eventually raised their four children.

Russ moved through the ranks to advance from sales to assistant manager, to branch manager, to assistant vice president and then finally to executive vice president responsible for Omaha's regional office, comprised of twenty branches throughout Nebraska.

One consequence of Russ's demanding career was travel. Sometimes he would need to be away for two weeks out of a month. While Melodie missed him very much, she knew he worked hard to provide for their family and he always showered her with gifts and love when he returned home.

She tolerated the travel, knowing that he was ensuring their comfortable retirement and hopefully an early retirement. And the kids certainly kept her occupied.

Zach told Russ he hated to pry into their personal financial situation, but needed to rule out any financial motives for which Russ would kill Melody and asked if the couple was in any financial trouble.

Russ responded "certainly not!" and that he worked hard to ensure their financial security now and in retirement. He left it at that, thinking Detective Willis didn't need to know any more than that unless asked.

Russ was quite proud of his financial savvy-it's what he did. He was in the right business and had the right tools at his disposal for planning retirement. He made hefty commissions and reinvested some of them with purchases of annuities through Challenge Life. Challenge Life was delighted to keep the funds within the company and it also provided some tax protection for him and Melodie. The annuities were for ten to twenty years into the future Therefore, his current income tax returns would properly reflect commissions income on a current basis, but not the income from the annuities since that income was deferred and would not be recognized for many years to come.

He traveled overseas often, into the Bahamas and Bermuda. While on business there, he opened accounts and would deposit cash there so that when he traveled he would always feel safe and secure with access to his funds as needed. It too, served as a tax shield for him and Melodie.

In addition to preparing for retirement, Russ also insisted they prepare for the unexpected. He and Melodie retained Jeffrey Maltzer as their estate attorney. Jeffery helped secure gifts to the children for their college funds and life insurance policies on both Russ and Melodie in the event that one of them were to die prematurely. They were well set.

He didn't think Detective Willis needed to know all that for now, unless he asked specifically.

"Detective Willis, sorry to interrupt", Susan the receptionist excused herself, "but the gentleman on the phone insists I put him through now."

"Damn. Excuse me a moment, Mr. Jenkins. I'll just get his name and number and call him back."

"I see", Zach said to the man interrupting their meeting, which Russ welcomed since it gave him time to reflect and think. "I am in an important meeting right now but I do need to speak with you further. Could you please call me back in a couple of hours?" Zach asked of the man who pushed his way through Susan to get to him. As he hung up, he apologized for the intrusion.

"Sorry about that Mr. Jenkins. Where were we?" Zach pressed on. "Oh yes, you were telling me about your marriage to Melodie.

"Melodie was the love of my life. She 'got me'; she was as driven as I was, so she understood my need to excel and she stayed out of my way and simply supported me in everything I set out to do. She was a unique combination of beauty, inside and out, with innocence and drive. That combination of personal characteristics is hard to come by in one woman, you know, Detective. She was everything to me. I don't know how to move on. I don't know how to stay strong for my kids. Melodie was RJ's strength and Beth's universe." Russ explained to the detective.

"It sounds all-American. Living the American dream, together. Was everything always this rosy between the two of you? Did you hit any rough patches?" Zach asked.

"Who doesn't?" Russ asked? "We were married twenty-two years! Things happen in that amount of time."

"Affairs?"

"Oh wow, Detective, you want to go there?"

"Yes, Russ. Were you or Melodie having an affair?" Zach insisted.

"No! No, neither of us was having an affair." Russ said firmly with an elevated tone.

Russ remained calm, knowing that this is standard questioning. He couldn't find out about his affair, because he was very cautious to never leave a paper trail. Then again, what if…what if…he found out? He felt a flush of heat from adrenaline, before reminding himself that even if his affair were discovered, affairs are not criminal.

"Thanks for stopping in, Russ. I'm sure we'll have more questions, so I'll be back in touch shortly."

"Detective," Russ began, as his face tightened and the corners of his mouth tensed and his teeth clenched, "my life has been turned upside down. My children's lives will never be the same. And Melodies' parents are beyond devastated. We all are. Detective Willis, we need you to bring this god-damned killer to justice as soon as possible. Now!"

Zach nodded, a gesture of assurance to Russ, as Russ left his office.

Chapter Eight

Russ thought back to how the affair got started again, and progressed into something serious around 1993. Russ had had a good day at work. A very good day. He'd been working on a large real estate giant for years, building his confidence in him while vying to earn his business. Finally, he got the call.

"Russ, Fred here. How are you today? I'm about to make your day even better. You earned my business, son. After three years you never gave up on me and continued to demonstrate that you put what is in the best interest of my family and me before your own. My finance guy ran out of chances. I'm not happy with how our investments are doing and I simply just don't like the guy. I'd love to meet you for dinner as soon as possible and talk about the details."

Fist pumping in the air, Russ could hardly keep control of his excitement. Calmly he responded, "Ah, Fred, thank you! Thank you! I will not let you down. I've promised my wife a hot date night tonight, but if tonight is the best night for you, I will cancel."

Fred responded, "Hey, I've been married long enough to know you cannot take away date night. Let's meet tomorrow night."

With that Russ accepted, and suggested Brother Sebastian's, the best steakhouse in Omaha at 6:30 the following night. "Looking forward to seeing you, Mr. Carlson. Yes, you did make my day. I will take good care of you and your family."

At only thirty-two years old, Russ was on track to already achieve a net worth of a million. "YES! YES! YES!" Russ hollered out loud.

He hopped into his silver BMW to head home. He couldn't wait to tell Melodie the good news when he got home. But first, he made a call. Damn! Voice mail. "Hey, it's me. You are not going to believe this! I just landed Carlson! We are having dinner tomorrow night at 6:30 to go over the details. We need to celebrate. This is huge! I'll email you, so check your email."

Russ made a quick stop at his bank's ATM to pull out three hundred dollars and headed home. Russ was surprised when he got home and Melodie had dinner just about done. She was so beautiful in her white and yellow flowered apron, with her hair pulled back into a pony tail and her glasses on, and seven months pregnant. Something about this woman still strikes him the way she did when he first met her. They were about to have their first child, which doctors expected to be a boy. They were absolutely delighted with the news and couldn't wait! With Russ's travel schedule, they were a both a bit concerned, but with Melodie's parents close by, they would be okay.

"Hi Princess! I thought I was going to take you out for a fancy date tonight?" he asked with a smile.

She explained that she didn't feel up to going out, but wanted to make a special night in with dinner and a movie, and even complete with popcorn. Sex was definitely off the table regardless, because she just couldn't get comfortable at that point. However, his hopes were up that perhaps she would take care of him. Especially after he told her his big news.

"Melodie, guess what? Do you remember Philip Moore? The real estate giant I've been trying to sell to for several years? He called today and said he's ready to do business with me. Melodie, this is huge! We are going to have a perfect life for little Russ. Unfortunately, I have to leave for the Bahamas tomorrow to meet with him to iron out the details. It'll be a fairly quick in and out trip; I need his original signatures. He wants his policies in place immediately" he apologetically explained to her.

"Oh my gosh, Russ, that is great news! I'm so proud of you. Don't worry about me. I'll be fine. I'll let my mom know you'll be out of town and she'll check on me. Now that I think of it, maybe I won't tell her because I won't have a silent moment to myself!" she giggled. Russ understood her need for peace and quiet, but he insisted she tell them she'll be alone for an overnight so they do check on her.

This was a great night for them. Russ opened the best red wine they had in the house to pair with the beef tips, roasted red peppers, while Melodie enjoyed the best sparkling water with a lemon twist in a wine glass.

After dinner, Russ had a lot to do for a last minute trip. He sent a quick email, "Hey, are you available tomorrow night? I have a client dinner tomorrow and I should be done by 8:30 and will go to the usual place. Can you meet me there?" Then he got busy packing and arranging his flight. He kept checking his email to see if he'd gotten a response and then finally he received confirmation, "Yes. See you there."

The movie and popcorn were great. Melodie wasn't in the mood for cuddling so he knew he wasn't going to get lucky and just got ready for bed. He knew he'd have a hard time sleeping, so he chased his wine down with a large dose of whiskey. That would help relax his mind so he could get some sleep and be fresh for the next day. And a busy day it would be!

The next morning, Russ filled his boss in on the great news about Fred Carlson and let him know he'd be closing the deal over dinner that night. Then he let him know that he had made some headway with his client in the Bahamas and would be going there the following day, and therefore would be out of the office. The whole office celebrated Russ's success with cheers and 'atta-boys' and firm pats on the back.

"Russ," Mr. Barnes said, "you have a long prosperous future here at Challenge Life. We have high hopes for you!"

Russ knew she would get to the hotel before he did so he put the room in her name: Jean Cameron. She arrived and checked in at the Holiday Inn Express. He always stayed at the Holiday Inn Express because it was easy to get in and out of and it was located outside the densely populated areas where no one knew him. The first thing she did was run a bubble bath. She had at least two hours before Russ arrived and she wanted to be absolutely irresistible to him. She soaked in the garden tub, which was spilling over with bubbles that smelled like pomegranate. Even though she'd already shaved her legs that morning, she shaved them again just to make sure they were silky smooth for him. She also carefully shaved her underarms and her bikini area then soaked in the bath, fantasizing about her times with Russ over so many years. He made her feel like no one ever could. He would bring her to orgasm over and over in one night. But for her, it was beyond the sex. She was devastated when he married Melodie. She never really got over it and was still envious of her. "It should be me with Russ!" she would say to herself on many occasions. She could never let go of him even if that meant she had to be the 'other woman'. Someday, he would leave his wife.

Jean slipped into an oversized 'boyfriend' button-down shirt, slathered lotion all over her arms and legs and stomach, avoiding 'kissable' areas to be sure the taste of the lotion wasn't a turn off to Russ. Her button-down shirt was unbuttoned to expose just enough of her breasts to be sexy but still covered. She had her stereo playing easy listening love songs playing in the background and had some wine already open and breathing. She was ready for him and eager. She was so hungry for him, it was all she could do to not get started without him. It had been nine weeks since she had last seen him. That was way too long. Once Melodie got pregnant, though, she was terrified he would break it off with her. He wanted to, because it was the right thing to do, but he just couldn't. He longed for her too much; she was too irresistible. And so were the other women that kept him satisfied. Jean was the only 'constant' girlfriend, though. Jean knew nothing of the other women.

Jean heard the sound of the key at the door and with that she got into position! She propped herself up on the bed with all the pillows behind her. She extended her left silky leg out in front of her, while the right one was bent at the knee, which exposed her lavender panties. Her shirt was just barely exposing her right breast.

"Oh my God. Look at you. You are beautiful!" Russ said with a beaming smile as he slid in next to her. He wrapped his arm around her waist pulling her close to him and they shared a long passionate kiss. His stubble scratched her face during their deep kiss, but Jean did not care. "I've missed you, Jean."

He noticed the wine and was in the mood to celebrate and tell her all about his dinner meeting, but first he had to take her. He had to have every delicate scent of her on him and he had to be inside her. They loved this hotel because the dresser with the mirror was positioned perfectly so they could watch themselves make love. They were both on their knees, with Russ behind her. She ran her fingernails across the back of his neck while he gently kissed her shoulder and neck. His right arm was draped across her chest caressing her breast while his left fingertips gently slid down inside her lavender panties. The image in the mirror was like a painting. They couldn't help but glance in the mirror watching themselves. If only they could capture that image forever.

He lasted as long as he could, making sure that Jean was well taken care of; twice already. It was finally time for him to just relax and let go. And Jean knew exactly what he liked and what set him over the edge. The love they made was stunningly beautiful, passionate and immensely satisfying.

"Jean, I have something to talk to you about" he began as he stepped over to the bar to retrieve the wine that had been patiently waiting since he arrived. "Listen, I'm headed to the Bahamas tomorrow to meet with a client. I wish you could go with me. I looked into booking a flight for you, but it's just too risky. That's a paper trail we really can't hide. What would you think about working for me at Challenger Life?

If you would like to be my Traveling Executive Assistant, you could fly on our company jets with me, no questions asked. Would you give that some thought?" Russ asked, or nearly begged.

"Well, let me see, Mr. Jenkins. There's a lot I have to sacrifice. I'll have to quit my current job, which I hate anyway. I'll have to listen to your jibber-jabber all day, which I love. I'll have to take orders from you, which could be fun. And, I might have to sleep with my boss to keep him happy and satisfied, which also could be fun. Okay, when do I start?" she playfully, but also seriously, responded.

"Jean, this could really work. Let me talk to my boss, Mr. Barnes, when I return from the Bahamas and see if he'll go for it. I landed this big account and just today he told me he sees a long prosperous career for me with Challenge Life. So, I think now is a good time to ask for something like this. And I know we can pay you at least ten grand more than you're making now."

"And don't you have a big account pending in the Bahamas, too? So that'll be an extra iron in your fire!" she reminded him.

"Oh yes, that one too. So many now I'm losing track!" he laughed.

Russ hit the ATM on the way to the airport to grab another $300 for travel cash. Once he arrived in the Bahamas, he retrieved his rental car and went straight to the Bank of the Bahamas to deposit most of his cash on hand. He had brought over $12,000 this time.

He loved the Bahamas! The weather was amazing and the beauty was breathtaking! And the bartenders were beautiful. Especially Sara. He definitely was going to see if Sara was working today. But first he had to try to make a few calls to see if any clients could see him on such short notice. He dialed a couple of numbers but only got voice-mails so he left messages introducing himself and Challenge Life. It would be great if someone called him back, but then again, it would also be great if no one did so he could enjoy all the Bahamas has to offer during his short trip. He felt he deserved to play a little hooky, since he had just landed this large account and worked far more than anyone else in the office. In actuality this was so true, that he really could have just told Mr. Barnes he wanted to take a day off and spend it in the Bahamas and he probably would have personally ordered him a Gully Wash for delivery right to his beach lounge!

Russ got settled in his hotel, and briskly changed into his shorts and tight T-shirt. He always wore tight T-Shirts to show off his well-toned physique. He grabbed his Oakley shades and caught a glimpse of himself in the full length mirror as he headed out to the Tiki Bar, pleased with what he saw.

"What'll ya have?" the tanned, sandy-blonde haired, buff bartender asked Russ. His name tag read 'Fillip'. His eyes were as crystal blue as he'd ever seen. He couldn't be much over 21.

"Hey, Fillip. How's it going? I'll have a Corona. So, is Sara working today?"

"Sara?" Fillip asks. "No man. She works over at the Daiquiri Shack now. Been there about three months. You a friend of hers?"

Russ was visibly disappointed. "Ah, damn. Well, just a good patron of hers. I'm here on business and she's always taken great care of me at the bar here."

It didn't take long for Russ to perk back up when Fillip went on to tell him, "Hey, she's working there tonight. Go over and say hello!"

And with that, Russ did. But first he thoroughly enjoyed his conversation with Fillip and took in the light breeze on the ocean side. Fillip was one of many locals who went to the Bahamas on vacation and just never went home. If only Russ had the free-living spirit to be able to do that. But with a wife and kids and high demands, he'd be working the white collar grind for a while; at least for another eleven years. He'd hoped to retire by fifty.

As always, Russ left a very good tip for Fillip and went on his way; a twenty-dollar tip for a fifteen-dollar tab.

Fillip smiled as he pocketed his tip, "Wow, this guy has a thing for Sara. Then again, who doesn't?" he thought.

He found his way to the Daiquiri Shack with no problem. He had been there plenty of times before, but it had been several months. He found a spot at the bar on the corner so he could make easy conversation with other patrons while also getting a great view of the ocean and TV. He waited patiently for Sara to notice him sitting there. She was a sexy kind of adorable. Tanned, of course, with dark shoulder-length hair braided in a loose French braid. It was kind of messy with several strands falling out of the hair tie she used to hold it all together. Then she had tiny butterfly clips, with sparkles scattered here and there. She wore very short tight jean shorts with a white belt. So hot. The bottom of her cheeks peeked out just slightly when she moved just a certain way. She wore a white ribbed tank with a red plaid button down shirt, tied in the front to expose her flat toned abs. She didn't have much to speak of 'up top', but just enough to have sex appeal.

Sara just couldn't move fast enough. The bar was a mad house. She tossed a beer down to the guy sitting next to Russ, and a Gully Wash to the girl on his other side, while taking another order from a lady already too drunk, but butting her way in to get attention. Finally, she glanced at Russ. "Hi! Sorry for the wait. Oh my God! Russ! What are you doing here? How long are you in town?" she asked with a huge smile, showing off her cute, crooked front tooth. Her smile was perfect, especially her one front tooth that sat at a slight angle making her smile unique and beautiful.

"So you do remember me?" he responded with a seductive laugh and a wink. He ordered a Jack on the rocks, and sipped it slowly, while watching her dance like a butterfly around the bar taking care of her patrons. This place was lucky to have gotten her!

"I'll have another when you have a moment!"

After finishing his second drink, he left her a big tip, along with the key to his room with the hotel name and room number. He disappeared before she could say goodbye but she discretely tucked the key in her front shorts pocket, tossed her tip in her tip jar and continued to flutter around the bar. She was a terrific multi-tasker. She never missed a beat at the bar while constantly daydreaming about the last time she was with Russ and fantasizing about what was to come that night.

Although he wasn't able to connect with any clients in the Bahamas this time, the trip was worth it. Not only was he able to make his deposit and discuss the future of his accounts with the Bank of Bahamas banker, he also got to spend some time with Sara. He would definitely miss seeing Sara as frequently when Jean started joining him on his trips, but they had no real connection. She was cute and fun, but just okay in bed and they had virtually nothing to talk about except her crazy customers at the bar.

Upon his return from the Bahamas, he spoke to Mr. Barnes about the need for a Traveling Assistant and said that he already had the perfect candidate in mind. Mr. Barnes quickly gave his approval and with that, Jeannette Cameron became Russ's Travel Executive Assistant, travel companion, girlfriend and lover, with a hefty salary of seventy-two thousand dollars a year.

Jean was absolutely delighted! Not only was she was going to make seventeen thousand more than she was making at her company where she was miserable, but more importantly, she would be with Russ during all of his travels! To help Jean with her transition to her new position, and her need for new clothes, travel gear and who knows what else, Russ gave her ten thousand dollars in cash to buy whatever she needed to get settled in her new job. He decided not to go through his company for her transition allowance because they had already agreed to great benefits and salary. Besides, ten thousand dollars was a small investment for Russ to make in his new assistant, to ensure she was prepared to look world class for his clients. He worked with big money people and she needed to look the part.

Chapter Nine

The medical examiner had the autopsy report ready for review. Melodie's cause of death was a single gunshot to the right temple. Her time of death was 7:00 a.m. If Russ's alibi checked out, he would have been in the Bahamas at that time and could be eliminated as a suspect.

"Joe, Zach here. Hey, ready to do some digging for me? Russ Jenkins claims to have been in the Bahamas since the night before Melodie was shot. Can you follow up on his alibi and make sure he was there when he said he was?"

"Sure thing. I live for this stuff! I'm on it." Joe assured Zach.

As soon as Zach hung up with Joe, his phone rang again. "Detective Willis? Hello, this is Christine from Forensics. I understand you are working the Jenkins case, correct?"

"Yes, Christine. Thanks for calling. What have you found out?"

"We are still running ballistics and searches for DNA from the crime scene which will take some more time. However, I did want you to know that we checked for semen or any other signs of sexual assault on your victim, and it came up negative. Your victim had no sexual activity before her murder."

"Thank you, Christine. I'll look forward to the rest of the forensics when the tests are done."

"That son of a bitch", Zach thought. "Russ just told me that he 'thanked God he got to make love to his wife before leaving for the Bahamas!' Even if he used a condom, which would be highly unlikely for a married couple their age, there would still be evidence of sexual activity. Russ had lied while looking me right in the eye." Zach knew he was on to something, however lying about having sex does not equate to murder. How many men, old and young, have lied about getting laid?

Chapter Ten

After leaving the station, Russ headed back to his home. On his way, his mind was racing. They are going to find out about the affair! Maybe he should have just come clean about that. But he just needed time to think. Besides, who is ever honest about an affair until all bets are off and the truth must be told? And just because I had an affair doesn't mean I murdered my wife!

He hadn't spoken with Jean since they returned from the Bahamas. His heart was aching for her, but he thought it was best to just not contact her for a little while.

He arrived home. He hadn't been there for two days, since the murder took place. It was surreal to pull up to the house. It looked so peaceful, like nothing had ever happened. He expected to walk in the door and be greeted by his wife and kids. Instead it was silent. It was deathly silent.

Less than one minute later there was a loud rap on the door. "Mr. Jenkins? Mr. Jenkins?"

Russ was reluctant to answer the door but somehow felt compelled to open it. "What can I do for you?" he asked in an indifferent tone, so the visitor knew she was interrupting at a bad time.

"Hello Mr. Jenkins. I am Kimberly of KPTM news. I'm sorry to hear about the loss of your wife. Do you know who might have wanted to hurt your wife?" she intruded.

"No, I do not!" he responded with a gruff voice as he slammed the door closed, but not before Kimberly shouted out one more question, "Did you kill your wife, Mr. Jenkins?"

As Russ walked through the house, he was flooded with memories. All the Thanksgivings and Christmas dinners in the dining room; Melodie getting lunches made for the kids every morning, year after year in the kitchen. RJ hated peanut butter; Elizabeth loved a mini Dove bar in every lunch; Ashley didn't like mayo, or was it mustard? How did Melodie keep it all straight? Somehow she always did.

The window was still broken in the back foyer where the killer broke in, which he'd have to take care of as soon as possible-definitely before his kids come back home from their grandparent's.

As he slowly moved one foot in front of the other to make his way up the stairs to the bedroom, he prayed that the cleaning service had already come in and cleaned all of the blood that may have been in the room. His heart was racing as he walked into the room as he remembered kissing Melodie in her sleep as he left for the Bahamas. He was relieved to see that it was cleaned. Thank God. Even the bed was freshly made; as if nothing ever happened and Melodie would walk in the door any minute.

The first call he made was to the glass repair company to replace the broken panel the intruder shattered to gain access into the home. After some heartfelt pleas, he was able to convince the company to squeeze in one more job at the end of the day. They would be there by 4:45 p.m.

The next call he made was to Melodie's parents to ask them to bring the kids back home at 8:00 p.m., if the kids felt up to being back home. That would give time for the glass to get repaired and for him to make the home feel as normal as possible.

The next call was to Jeffery Maltzer, their estate attorney. "Hello Jeff. Russ here."

"Russ, hello. God, I'm sorry to hear about Melodie. Have they caught the bastard?" he asked with genuine sincerity.

"Not yet, Jeff. I'm praying they do it fast. So, as much as I wish I never had to ask this, I need to find out how the life insurance will work in this situation. I know Melodie and I prepared for something like this, hoping it would never happen, and we have policies to protect each child in the event of one of our deaths. I think each child has a one-million-dollar benefit. How will they have access to these funds?"

"It's actually three-million per child, Russ. Three-million. That's a lot of money!" Jeffery corrected. "I'll get back with you within the next few days to let you know what the procedure is."

Russ had to call the funeral home. Melodie and Russ did a great deal of planning, so thank God, this would be the easy part. They already had the funeral home chosen along with the casket and burial plot. Russ only had to make the call and set the plan in motion. The funeral would be Saturday, in only two days. This was becoming all too real.

As Russ straightened up the kids' rooms to prepare for their return home, and wanting everything to seem as normal as possible, his phone rang. 'Damn. This is going to be non-stop!' he thought as he debated whether to answer it or not. "Hello?"

"Hey my love. I just wanted to see how you're doing." Jean was on the other end. She shouldn't have called! However, she really was his work colleague and she was traveling with him on business when they got the news. So, it would be natural, under any circumstance, for her to check on him.

"God, I miss you Jean. I'm hanging in there, but I'm really worried about the kids. They are coming home tonight and I'm trying to get everything ready for them. Sorry I haven't called. You know, it just doesn't look good." Russ began to explain.

"I know, I know. Don't you worry about me. What have the police said about who they think may have done this?"

"I met with them this morning and they needed to eliminate me as a suspect first. They know I was in the Bahamas at the time of her murder, but as I left, they asked if either of us was having an affair. I lied, Jean. I didn't know how to say 'yes, but I didn't kill my wife.' I know they are going to find out in no time, and I'm sure they'll be calling you soon. They have no suspects yet."

"Russ, don't worry. Like you said, it doesn't mean you could. I can't even say it, Russ! I need to see you. When can I see you?"

"Soon, Jean, soon. I have to run for now. I miss you and love you. Hang in there."

The glass people were late, but at least they showed up. No one ever comes on time anymore, and they did squeeze in Russ's job today so he couldn't complain. The house now looked like nothing ever happened. The kids' rooms were cleaned, beds made, everything put away. RJ still had a room there although he wasn't home often anymore. Russ wanted to make sure their bedrooms were not as they left them when they went to their grandparents to minimize triggers of their last moments with their mother. He put on the Avengers, which all the kids liked. Ashley was in love with Thor and RJ idolized Iron Man. Elizabeth was a huge fan of Scarlett Johansson and she loved any movie in which Scarlett performed. So did Russ. And Kimberly thought Captain America looked ridiculous in that outfit they made him wear, but she thought he had the cutest smile and loved the shield.

Like clockwork, Charles and Elizabeth had the children home right on time at 8:00 p.m. They came inside and besides pleasant 'hellos', no words were spoken among the adults. Just huge hugs. Charles hugged Russ as they both held back tears, trying to be strong for the kids. Melodie's mother hugged Russ and could not hide the tears, but she managed not to cry out loud.

Finally, they assured Russ that the kids had eaten for the evening, of course, but RJ was ready for a snack. They told Russ that the kids hadn't really asked anything about their mother. They'd been quiet; they hadn't had the TV on except for movies to avoid any news coverage. They also were able to schedule a session with a therapist the day after tomorrow. They thought that would be good so they can first talk with their father about their feelings, questions and even process the fact that their mother wasn't coming home.

The kids entered the home bickering about something, like normal. They each eked out a quick "Hi Dad" as they went to their rooms.

"Cool! Avengers!" RJ said as he whisked past the 65" TV on his way to his room.

Melodie's parents said their goodbyes for the night and Russ started some popcorn. Tonight surely called for extra butter and plenty of salt.

"Kids come on out and watch Avengers with me!" Russ pleaded. Then he heard a shriek from one of the girls' rooms.

"Oh my God, Dad! Who touched my stuff! What did you do? How dare you, or anyone, touch my stuff!" That was Ashley, the fifteen-year-old, freaking out because her privacy had been totally invaded by an adult trying to do something nice and clean her room for her. "Mom would never do that to me!" she continued.

Russ went to her room to calm her down. "Honey, I'm sorry. Not only was I trying to do something nice for you, so you'd come home to a clean room, but honey, I needed to do something. I don't know what to do now with every minute that passes, but we're going to figure it out together. I won't do it again, I promise." he assured her. Ashley calmed down and apologized to him and went over to hug him. "Dad, don't worry. Mom is coming home."

The house was filled with the fresh smell of popcorn. Russ gathered the kids and encouraged them to stay together in the family room, and with a little coaxing, he was successful. RJ was pretty much a recluse so the only thing that could get him out of his room was a

good Super Hero movie. Other than that, he stayed in his room playing video games or just lying on his bed, daydreaming about who-
knows-what, staring at the ceiling. They forbade a TV in his room, or
they would never get him out when he came home.

"Captain America looks so gay in that outfit!" Kimberly sighed.
At thirteen, she was already the fashion police in the Jenkins household, and at school, the mall, everywhere she went.

Russ gathered the popcorn bowls. These were the fun movie night
popcorn bowls with red and white stripes and the words 'popcorn
and a movie' painted in playful print. They only had four though, so
Russ grabbed himself a regular cereal bowl. They started the movie
over from the beginning and as expected, the only people still awake
at the end were RJ and Ashley. They poked and teased at the other
family members when it was over to tell them to go to bed!

Everyone scurried off to their bathrooms to get ready for bed,
changed into their pajamas and called it a night. Russ went to each
room to kiss the kids good night and to tell them he loved them.
He assured each one of them that he'd be there for them when they
had questions or wanted to talk. The girls all said, "Thanks Dad, but
I'm fine. Everything is fine." RJ, on the other hand got belligerent.
"Quit talking like that, Dad! Mom is coming home! Nothing bad happened to her! You don't know what you're talking about!" Russ didn't
know how to respond to that, so he tried to hug him, and RJ violently
pushed him away and screamed, "Don't touch me!" Russ simply said,
"I'm sorry RJ. I love you. Everything is going to be okay."

The girls all heard the scuffle but ignored it.

At 3:00 in the morning, little Beth snuck into Russ's room and climbed up into bed with him. She had the teddy bear with her that Melodie had given her when she was only five years old. She'd never let any new stuffed animal of any kind replace that little bear, even as she grew older. He kissed her forehead and she began to cry. "Daddy, Mommy's just gone away for a little while, right? You just said mean things yesterday. She's coming home. I know she is!"

"Beth, oh God how I wish she were. Honey, Mommy is in heaven now. She's with God. She loves you so much and she will always be watching from heaven." He tried comforting her.

"No, Daddy, no! That just cannot be. She was just here with us. She got us ready for our slumber party at Grandma and Pa's. You're wrong! You're just wrong!" she sobbed.

He just held her tightly until she cried herself to sleep.

Chapter Eleven

Early the next morning, Zach was informed that the results of the initial investigation were in. The back foyer window was broken, showing forced entry. However, the glass shards fell outside rather than inside, leading to the conclusion that the killer staged the scene to make it look like an intruder entered through the back foyer door. So, either Russ left the house unlocked when he left for the Bahamas that morning, or the killer was someone they knew who had access to the home.

From the blood splatter and position of Melodie's body, it was clear she was shot while she was still sleeping. There were no foreign prints in the home. The home was ransacked but no valuables were missing. The drawers in the bedroom were pulled out, and the clothes were disheveled, but not dumped onto the floor. That was inconsistent with robbery. Typically, burglars will dump the drawers or at least thrust everything from a drawer to the floor to ensure no valuables are left unseen. It's possible the robbers knew what they were looking for, so perhaps a thorough ransacking wasn't necessary, but that was unlikely. It appeared that the scene was staged to look like a robbery. Melodie also had no signs of rape, so a sexual assault was ruled out. The DNA testing was back and all of the blood found on the scene was from Melodie. There just wasn't much to go on.

Joe, Zach's investigator, also couldn't find any proof that Russ was on any flight from Omaha to the Bahamas that night, that morning, or ever. For as many trips as he took to the Bahamas and Bermuda, how could there be no flight records for him?

Zach needed to ask Russ a few more questions.

The doorbell rang, and Kimberly was the first one to holler, "I'll get it!" as she sprinted to the door, certain it would be her mom coming home. Russ tried to stop her, but she was too fast. She flung open the door and two tall men were at the door. One was in a uniform and the other was in regular street clothes.

"Good morning. Is your dad...."

"Seriously, Zach, I haven't even had a full cup of coffee yet." Russ scolded. "Kimberly, go eat your breakfast." He then turned his attention back to Zach and the officer. "I hope you have some promising information for me, but now is not the best time to discuss this", he whispered as he signaled that his kids were up and present.

"I apologize, Mr. Jenkins. I know it's early. Can you come by the station later today where we can speak more freely?"

"I'll need to see if my in-laws are available to come stay with the kids. I'm not sending them back to school yet", he replied.

As Russ closed the door, Ashley softly asked, "Dad, did they find mom? What'd they say?" All three sweet girls, faces of innocence, eyes of hope, were staring at him, hoping the people at the door were their superheroes today and their knight in shining armor was about to give them the good news.

"Girls…Ashley, Kimberly, Beth, I love you more that I can ever say. I am so sorry. I'm so sorry. Your mother is not coming home again. I was truthful to you at Grandma and Grandpa's. I wish it weren't true. I want to see her walk in the front door, too, but to hang on to that hope is just not healthy." Russ's heart was broken for his girls. Oh, how their cries were unbearable! How he loved those girls. Kimberly lost control and began punching her dad on the chest screaming 'No! No! You are lying! She's okay!' and then would hug him so tight with her face buried into the very place she just punched him repeatedly.

"Girls, mom's funeral is Saturday. The funeral home would like to make a presentation to show all of our favorite pictures of mom on their TVs. Would you like to find your favorite pictures and save them to a thumb drive and we'll get them to the funeral home? Also, pick out what you'd like to wear. You can wear whatever you want, but just remember this will be a lifetime memory for you, so you might want to wear a dress, or something mom got for you and that you love" Russ suggested.

"I'll help them, Dad", Kimberly proclaimed.

"The hell you will!" Ashley quickly denied her the opportunity.

"Hey! Ashley, don't talk like that!" Russ was quickly losing control of his household. He had never heard Ashley speak like that before.

Kimberly was delighted when Beth asked her for help picking out the perfect outfit.

Of course, there was no chance RJ would go to the funeral. Russ went to his room to check on him.

"Hey, RJ. How're you doing?"

"Get out!" he shouted back to his dad.

Russ entered to find RJ lying on his bed staring at the ceiling, fiddling with his wrist. He noticed some blood peeking through on his wrist. "Hey, what's going on here, RJ?" he asked as he saw that RJ had picked the skin from his wrist causing it to bleed. "Nothing. Get the hell out!" RJ demanded.

Russ went to get a clean damp cloth with some peroxide. "I'll just leave this here for you. I'm here for you. I love you, RJ". Hearing no response, Russ quietly closed the door to give him his privacy.

Oh, how he needed the therapist's help! That appointment couldn't come soon enough. He had no idea what to say and how to handle their pain and confusion.

Russ contacted his in-laws to ask if they would be available to come to the house to stay with the kids while he took care of the things that needing tending to (including another trip to the police station).

Before heading to the police station, he took a little detour, near downtown Omaha to Jean's condo. He wasn't sure if she was going to be home, but he wanted to call as little as possible, knowing the police would be taking a look at his cell phone records. So, he thought he'd just surprise her. She had a beautiful condo with a garage. Of course, Russ had a key and a garage door opener. When he arrived, he hit the garage door opener he kept hidden in the console of his car. Her new red Corvette was sitting in the garage. She sure looked smokin' hot in that car! Especially with the top down. He was relieved she was home; he was aching for her touch.

She was overjoyed to see him and ran to him as he opened the door. She was just getting ready to hit the treadmill, which reminded him that it had been several days since he'd worked out and he was beginning to feel sluggish! He made a commitment to himself to start running again the next morning.

Once her condo door was completely closed, Jean gave him the most passionate kiss. God, did he need it! He needed her passion. But, he surely didn't have time to make love today; he just had to see her. He explained he was on his way to the police station, then the funeral home, then to meet with the insurance agent.

"Russ, please stay with me tonight. I need you. The kids have their grandparents with them. Stay here with me, please" Jean begged.

"Come on, Jean. You know I cannot do that. You know I love you, but my family is turned upside down right now and the police are watching my every move. I'm praying they didn't follow me over here right now! Be patient, my love," he insisted.

She couldn't help herself but to ask him what the future was going to be like for them now that Melodie was gone. At first, Russ scowled at the question, but then gently took her by her waist and pulled her into him, looking deeply into her eyes and told her, "I can't answer that right now, but I can tell you I love you. Right now I can't think about, or make any promises, to you or anyone of what the future is."

Jean tried to understand but deep down, she was devastated. She always fantasized that if Melodie was not in the picture that she and Russ would be together. He was right, though; she had to remain patient.

Russ really did love her. He wanted to move her into their home on 196th now! But that would be catastrophic for his family and it surely would not look good to the authorities. He needed to keep Jean thinking clearly and not getting her hopes up for any changes in their relationship, and especially their living arrangements too soon. He had only twenty minutes to get to the station. He had to go, as difficult as it was to say goodbye, for now.

Traffic today sucked. By the time he arrived at the station to talk with Zach again, he was already frustrated. He knew he had to calm down to have the patience to deal with the questioning. He knew he had to cooperate whole-heartedly or he would wind up a suspect. So, he took three very deep breaths, in through his nose, held for four counts, and exhaled through his mouth. It's amazing how well that works. Now mentally prepared to deal with Zach, he confidently walked through the door of the station and asked to see the detective.

"Hello. I'm here to see Detective Willis. He is expecting me, Russ Jenkins." he announced to the receptionist. He didn't have to wait at all; before Susan could call back to Zach's office, Zach saw him and came out to greet him.

"Mr. Jenkins! Good afternoon. Thank you for coming in. We have just a couple questions we need your help with. This won't take more than ten minutes."

Russ was the first one to ask questions, "Detective Willis, what have you found out? I hope to God you have a suspect or at least a person of interest."

"Don't worry, Mr. Jenkins, we are close. We promise you that. First, you know we need to clear you completely and something odd came up during our investigation of your alibi. I'm sure you can explain it away for us. Mr. Jenkins, all flights to The Bahamas from Omaha were checked out, and we were not able to place you on any flight. Not only the day of the murder, but any day. I know you go there often. Are you driving to Florida then swimming to the Bahamas?" he asked with a chuckle.

"Now that would be a great workout! I might try that sometime! Okay, seriously, no Detective. I take the company jet. We have a Gulfstream 4 and when I need to fly on business, they almost always have me take the G-4, unless someone else already has it booked. I guess now that I think of it, I haven't ever had to take a commercial airline to the Bahamas." Russ explained.

"Now that's the life! I'm in the wrong occupation, Russ!" Zach laughed.

"Oh no you're not! The community needs you tracking down these thugs!" Russ said, admittedly intending to flatter him a little bit.

"I'll keep you informed, Russ. Thanks again for stopping in." Zach and Russ shook hands, nodded and Russ departed.

After a quick call to Joe, and a visit to Challenge Life, Zach was able to confirm that Russ did indeed take the G-4 to the Bahamas at 6:00 in the morning. In addition, his Traveling Executive Assistant, Jean Cameron, was with him, thus his alibi checked out. He was eliminated as a suspect. They needed to learn a little bit more about Miss Cameron, though.

Jean was very nervous when the detectives showed up at her door. She was trembling inside, but she held it together and was shocked when they were only there to ask about Russ's statement of being in the Bahamas with her at the time of Melodie's murder. They asked the nature of their relationship and she simply stated that she worked with him and was his Executive Traveling Assistant. She wanted to add something funny to cut the tension such as, "Russ can't find his way out of a paper bag without an assistant", but she was too nervous to add anything that was not specifically asked of her. They thanked her for her time and left.

When they left, she was so overwhelmed with relief that she had to do a nice hard shot of Jack to calm her nerves. She was shaking uncontrollably, but thank goodness, she held herself together during their visit. She was too shaken up to even call Russ, so she would text him. Her hands were trembling too much to text. Maybe another shot of Jack would do the trick. She thought she'd give that a whirl and then just sit down and try to relax. 'Oh my God. What have I gotten myself into?' she whispered to herself. She cupped her face into her trembling hands and began to cry, and this quickly turned to sobs.

As Russ was driving home from the station, his phone rang. Before he could even say hello, as soon as the phone stopped ringing, the caller came bellowing through, "What the hell, Russ?"

"Good morning to you, too, Sharon", Russ responded with a tinge of sarcasm.

"Russ, I've been waiting for you to call me to tell me what the hell is going on with Melodie. As your divorce lawyer, I'm going to be questioned by the police. What happened? And please, God, tell me you had nothing to do with it! I know you couldn't..."

Russ cut her off, mostly to calm her down because she was talking herself into a frenzy. "Sharon, of course I had nothing to do with it! I was in the Bahamas to meet with a client at the time of her death and the police were able to verify that. I'm sorry I hadn't called; I was more concerned with my kids, the funeral arrangements, and I have been busy with the police trying to help them find the suspect, or shall I say, rule me out as a suspect so they can start looking for a real suspect or at least a person of interest."

He went on to tell her that the kids were not only struggling with how to deal with the loss of their mother, but they were actually in denial. They kept saying she was going to walk through the door any time. Every time the police called, they hoped it's to tell them they found their mother and she's going to be okay. RJ, understandably, was doing the worst. His world was crumbling around him without his mother and his autism prevented him from having coping skills. Russ hoped the funeral would provide some sense of closure so they could begin working with the psychologist in a meaningful way.

"Russ, do you think Jean had anything to do with this?" she asked. Sharon and Mr. Haroldson, Melodie's divorce attorney, were the only ones who knew about the affair with Jean.

"God, no. She was with me, in the Bahamas, meeting with clients," he assured her.

She continued with her questions. "Do the police know you were starting divorce proceedings?"

"It does not seem like they do. I've been in for questioning a couple times, and it's never come up."

Like most opposing divorce lawyers, Sharon Means had little love for Harvey Haroldson. Harvey felt the same way about Sharon.

When Melodie found out about Russ's affair with Jean, she filed for divorce immediately and hired Mr. Haroldson. Mr. Haroldson was one of the top divorce attorneys in Douglas County and Harvey quickly summed up Russ as an unfaithful liar, cheating on Melodie every chance he had, with his work as his excuse. He'd had to deal with far too many assholes like Russ! They give up their entire lives, destroy the lives of their children, and betray everyone who loves them, to just get a little extra something-something on the side. Selfish assholes.

Sharon, also a leading lawyer in Douglas County, defended Russ's actions because Melodie did not give Russ the attention and affection he needed. What did she expect? Men have needs and their needs are going to be met—either at home with their wives, or elsewhere, if necessary. Men are testosterone filled providers and sexual fulfillment is wired into their DNA. Every woman knows that.

Chapter Twelve

Melodie's funeral was held at the Rambo Funeral Home. Russ arrived with the girls an hour early, knowing they would need extra time to internalize the truth of what happened and say goodbye to their mother.

Kimberly was delighted that Elizabeth accepted her help with picking out the perfect dress for mom. The most important factor was for Beth to pick out a dress that mom had given her and she started with that. The dress was pink with dainty white flowers along the bust line and spaghetti straps. The length was just to her knee and the fabric was, as Ashley puts it, fluffy; so it moved happily with her. The problem was that she needed something to cover her shoulders and she needed accessories. She was delighted when her grandmother took her shopping for a cute three-quarter sleeve sweater that was made just to cover shoulders. It was perfect! She also found a white purse with a pink flower on the front and beautiful pink hair clip.

She looked adorable, Kimberly thought. She was very proud of her masterpiece!

She thought Ashley's black dress was boring and distasteful, but there wasn't any changing her mind.

And, of course, Kimberly was dressed to turn heads, with the perfect color palette in blues (not too cheery for a funeral, like yellow; yet not too gloomy like black) with perfect complementary accessories from the clutch to the earrings.

RJ refused to go. Russ could not get him to even leave his room. It broke Russ's heart knowing that this was the last chance for him to say goodbye to his mother, but he was angry, belligerent and there just was no convincing him.

The funeral home was originally built in 1842 with breathtaking architecture. The two-story magnificent building stood tall on a hill of rolling green grass and evergreen trees lining the west border of the two-acre property. The entrance was embraced by a huge front porch with solid yet creaky wood slats. The double doors were filled with stained glass, which opened up to a massive spiral staircase, delicately laid with oriental runners and oak handrails.

To the left of the entrance was the social room with a majestic organ. A woman of at least seventy-five years of age was playing the organ, striking every key with intensity that felt like agony but sounded like heaven. Several antique sofas, chairs, coffee tables and end tables with antique lamps filled the seating space. A hand carved oak desk with a hand carved chair, carefully tucked into it, sat at the end of the room. While the desk and chair were beautiful, they were clearly out of place with their modern design.

To the right of the entrance was a drawing room where the funeral services take place. Instead of benches stretching across the space like pews, mahogany wooden folded chairs with ivory striped built-in cushions lined the sitting area. A huge oriental area rug, which matched the runner on the spiral staircase, was used as the warming accent to soften the space. Under the area rugs was the original creaking wood.

The scent of carnations, lilies, gladioli, and chrysanthemums filled the whole home. Flowers accented the spiral staircase, lined the social area, and led to Melodie's casket. The Farnsworth's must have bought every flower available in Omaha for their little girl. Her casket was draped with a spray of pure white lilies, gladioli and carnations. Countless easels propped up more flowers, one spelling out "MOM" that Russ helped the kids pick out; and many others from friends and family.

The mortician did an amazing job on Melodie. Even with a gunshot wound to her head, they were able to have an open casket. This was important for the kids to really be able to say goodbye to their mother, and also to begin to integrate the fact that she was not coming back.

All of the children went to pieces when they saw their mother's lifeless body lying in the casket. Russ stayed strong, and once again made sure they each knew how much Melodie loved them. After about twenty minutes, it all became surreal to them. Their tears had dried, for now, and they were fascinated with the makeup applied to their mother. It's so much! She never wore that much makeup!

Jean arrived, looking beautiful. She was in a conservative black dress with long sleeves and a scoop neckline. She wore a delicate string of pearls with a matching bracelet. Her black heels were a moderate height, to give her a little lift, yet still perfectly classy for the occasion. She wore her hair down with soft big curls.

Russ could tell she had arrived just by her scent that filled the air.

"Oh, Russ, I'm so terribly sorry about Melodie", she consoled.

"Thank you" he responded, as they hugged briefly. "I still just can't believe it." As they let go of their comforting hug, their eyes met and without saying a word Russ could see the worry for him in Jean's eyes and Jean could see the fear in Russ's. They had so much history together, from their college years to working together now, they could have an entire conversation without saying a word.

The girls ran to Jean. "Miss Cameron! You're here!" They all hugged tightly as Jean reassured the girls that their mother loved them very much and will be looking over them at every moment. Russ was relieved to see the girls accepting Jean's comfort. Not knowing how to help the kids cope, having another motherly figure was just what he needed for them.

"Russ, if you or your kids need me for anything-and I mean anything-please call me. I can help you get them to school, or just to play games or pack lunches. Seriously, please let me know if I can help in any way" Jean insisted.

"Whoa, be careful what you offer, Miss Cameron! You just may get a second full time job!" Russ teased. "We do appreciate your kind offer. I will be sure to call you if we need a hand."

Of course, Zach was at the funeral too, watching those who came to pay their respects. He was watching for anyone who behaved suspiciously, such as obsessing over the details of the case; or keeping to him or herself without interacting with anyone. He was particularly paying close attention to Russ, the grieving husband. Sure, his alibi checked out and he was in the Bahamas, but could he have hired someone to kill his wife? Joe was staking out the scene from his car, watching for slow passersby to see if anyone may be curious about Melodie's funeral, but not actually attend.

Zach's phone began to vibrate. He stepped aside to answer. "Joe. What's up?"

Joe spotted a tall thin man walking very slowly past the funeral home. He was dressed in black jeans, a black hoodie pulled up, with both hands tucked in his pockets. The whole time he walked past the funeral home, he stared at it, without taking his eyes off it, as if he were looking for someone. It wasn't until he got far enough past the building that he finally looked forward again, although staring down at his feet as he walked.

"Zach, he definitely had an interest in what was going on in the funeral home. I'll keep an eye on him. I took pictures, but never saw his face." "Alright Joe. Stay on it."

Joe did just that, never taking his eyes off the suspiciously behaving passerby. The man just sauntered down the street until almost out of sight. Of course, Joe never went anywhere without his 'binocs', as he called them, so looking through his trusted binoculars, he could keep tracking his suspect. He went into a convenience store, spent no more than five minutes in there, and was on his way back towards Joe. Whatever he bought at the store, if anything, was small enough to fit in his pocket.

Now that he was headed back his way, he could get a look at his face this time. Joe was ready with his fancy zoom lens, if only the son-of-a-bitch would quit looking at the ground and look the hell up! "Dammit, kid, look up!" Joe grunted out loud, but no one was around to hear him. "Thank the Lord! Finally!" A quick look up and Joe snapped as many pictures his camera could take in a matter of two seconds. He was a white kid, either in his late teens or early twenties. He couldn't see his hair, but from a distance through his lens, it looked like he had brown eyebrows and facial hair. He had a five-day shadow working and was definitely simply unshaven. He couldn't tell the eye color yet. He looked a bit rough, probably a smoker, maybe did some drugs. He definitely didn't look like he fit into this part of town.

As the kid approached the funeral home, his eyes were glued to it once again, staring into the home without taking his eyes off of it while managing to dial Zach.

"Zach, you might want to come talk to this kid. He's about to approach the funeral home again."

The kid was only a few steps beyond the funeral home and Joe and Zach approached him.

"Excuse me! Excuse me, young man! Wait up!" Zach hollered to get his attention.

"Whadya want?" he asked, clearly annoyed.

"What's your fascination with this funeral home?"

First, the response was "nothing" and to leave him alone. He just needed to go to the store. He tried denying that he even looked at the funeral home. However, after flashing the badge and asking if he knew what the penalty was for lying to a police officer, he finally decided to explain himself.

The kid's story was that his mother had passed away a month ago and the funeral was held here, at the same funeral home where Melodie's was. The kid was so distraught over his mother's death, he couldn't bring himself to go to the funeral, a decision he has regretted ever since. By the time he finished explaining himself, tears ran down his cheeks like a running stream. Zach and Joe were heartbroken for the kid and offered to take him home, but he preferred to walk.

Joe made a few calls to verify the young man's story and it all checked out. Still, no suspects.

Zach had done all he could do during the service, so he was ready to head out. Meanwhile, the Farnsworths wanted to take the kids home with them after the funeral, which Russ welcomed. He still had a great deal to take care of. He could use Jean's help, so Russ suggested she follow him back to his place. He had mountains of paperwork to go through in his office and they needed to discuss the management of his Challenge Life accounts while he was out, taking care of his personal business.

Jean's heart was fluttering at the invitation. She didn't have other clothes to change into but for Russ to invite her back to his home he shared with his family was just what Jean wanted. It was what she'd been waiting for. She didn't care that she didn't have a change of clothes or even an overnight bag. She was praying she would go to sleep next to Russ and wake up next to him in the morning.

Chapter Thirteen

It had been four weeks since the murder. Zach and the other officers had questioned all of the neighbors and no one had seen or heard anything unusual at all the morning of Melodie's murder. They dusted for prints and found only the family's prints along with Glaucia's in the home. There were no shoe prints, foot prints or palm prints. And they never found the gun or even the casings. They had nothing. "NOTHING, DAMMIT!" Zach bellowed as he slammed the case files shut and tossed it in the legal box labeled 'Melodie Jenkins'.

"Somehow this bastard killed his wife! He's running around with his Executive Traveling Assistant and something just ain't right about him. I know it, dammit, I know it! But I've got nothing!"

Zach had had tough cases before and he had always solved them. This was the first one he was losing sleep over. Night after night; week after week; month after month.

Six months had passed, and Zach went to the holding room where all the case files were held to retrieve Melodie's again. As he passed various cases, some still had a grasping hold on him—cases he'd solved over time. Donny Reynolds, the seventeen-year-old kid who got stabbed to death in what ended up being a simple mistaken identity incident. Some thug wanted retaliation for stealing drugs. It appeared this guy operated by the rule of thumb of 'stab first, ask questions later'. Donny was just walking home from a friend's house. It was late, around 10:30, on a school night. He and his friend were cramming to finish their science projects together. "Thumper", he's called on the streets, walked up, switchblade already popped, and stabbed the kid in the abdomen, piercing his kidney. The crime was so random, and the streets wouldn't talk. It took five weeks, but he refused to let Donny's mother down and he promised to get justice for her only son. He would never forget that case. Such a useless killing. It's Donny's case that reminds him to kiss and hug his kids good night, good morning, and every chance he can. And, to never let them walk home alone at night—ever.

Jane Stella Johnson—closed; Wayne Drummond—closed; Melodie Jenkins—open.

Zach started all over, reviewing every photograph to see what he possibly could have missed. Every log, every interview. Every photo. Something about Russ's alibi just was not sitting well with him. "That SOB had to have killed his wife!" he said to himself, through clenched teeth, while studying the photo of Melodie's lifeless body, paying particular attention to the pool of blood surrounding her once beautiful face and gorgeous long red hair. He gazed at the picture, focusing every thought on what it must've been like at that given moment. Thinking, if the intruder gained access by breaking the downstairs window, why hadn't she awakened from the sound? Why would she still be lying in bed? The glass shards were strewn more outside than inside, proving it was broken from the inside, not the outside. That was staged. But, who would Russ have hired to kill her? His phone records showed no unusual activities, nor did his email activity. No money was wired or transferred from his accounts. "C'mon, Melodie, tell me! How did Russ kill you?" he asked, expecting an answer.

A rush of adrenaline filled his body. He felt tingly from head to toe. "The time of death may be correct, but not the… Yes, I've got that son of a bitch!" he bellowed! "I'll be back", as if anyone was listening at the station, "I need to talk to the DA."

Melodie's parents were devastated all over again, but they also could not go on without having justice for their daughter. They were appreciative that Detective Willis was doing anything and everything he needed to do to put this psychopath behind bars forever. Zach did not tell them that Russ was his suspect; he simply told them they needed to verify the time of death one more time, so previously 'ruled-out suspects' may be reconsidered. Charles and Elizabeth were very smart people—they got a heart-wrenching feeling in their gut that Detective Willis suspected Russ and they could not accept that. They knew he was wrong.

Four hours later, Zach received a call from Russ. Oh, how he did not want to answer that call. After three full rings, Zach finally hit 'talk'. "Hello Mr. Jenkins. How are you this afternoon?" he managed to ask in a confident, upbeat voice, knowing what would follow.

"Who the hell do you think you are, exhuming Melodie's body?" Russ screamed almost uncontrollably.

"Mr. Jenkins, if you want us to catch your wife's killer, we need to take another look. New evidence has come forward and we need to confirm the new evidence with the facts of the case. Listen, I understand how traumatic this is for you and Melodie's parents, and I am deeply sorry for that. But, Russ, we need to catch this guy."

After several minutes of arguing, and Zach letting Russ know the court order was already in process, Russ hung up on Zach. Zach leaned back in his chair, trying to hold back a faint smile and whispered to himself "what are you trying to hide, Mr. Jenkins?"

The following three weeks seemed like an eternity to the family, but Zach was busy with a forensic pathologist, medical experts, other experts, and re-interviewing everyone already interviewed previously, except for Russ. Sometimes after an initial interview, someone may remember some other detail, but not think it's important enough to contact the police to report. Perhaps a neighbor remembered hearing something unusual, or saw someone in the neighborhood who didn't belong, or some other seemingly unimportant detail.

They also combed through Russ's alibi all over again. He had a date with Melodie the night before she was murdered. The kids were at their grandparents. He kissed her goodbye, while she was still sleeping, at 4 a.m. and flew out to the Bahamas at 5 a.m. on the company's GulfStream 4. All of this checked out. Melodie's time of death was reported as 7 a.m.

The forensic pathologist was given strict instructions for the second exam: it is the time of death that is in question. Could there have been an error? Could she have died before 7 a.m.? Is it possible the time of death could be between 4 a.m. and 6 a.m.? To be sure not to bias the examination, no other theories were shared with the doctor.

The decomposition of her body was not too extensive, but still, conducting an examination on an exhumed body was not easy for the pathologist, Rebecca to stomach. She just kept a clear vision on what got her into this line of work and remembered she was there to make sure justice is granted for every victim, in memory of her boyfriend when she was a teenager. Now in her thirties, she was married and had two beautiful children, but every day she goes to work, she says a prayer for Jimmy and every victim and their families. She needed to be sure her first examination didn't miss anything to ensure Melodie and her family get the justice they need, deserve and demand.

After three hours, Rebecca still felt confident that the time of death was correct on the first examination. Rigor mortis typically occurs beginning two hours after death. When the housekeeper found Melodie, dead in her bedroom, it was just after 8 a.m. and rigor mortis had not yet set in. It was approximately 9:07 when it began. Rebecca had made another observation, however, and completed her examination. Moments later, she phoned Zach.

"Zach, hey, it's Rebecca. You wanted me to contact you after I completed my examination of Jenkins. Listen, I'm confident that the time of death is accurate at 7 a.m.", she reported.

"Did you..." he began, but Rebecca cut him off to finish her thought.

"However, the time of death and the time of incident do not appear to be the same! Zach, at the time of death, the heart stops pumping and the blood is 'unfixed', meaning the blood will flow towards whatever position the body is in. Prior to death, of course, blood is pumping and the body immediately begins to work hard to heal any injury. The bullet wound in Jenkins' head showed signs of healing, or blood clotting. The only way for this to happen would be if she was shot and then laid unconscious for a few hours prior to her passing. If she died at the time of the shooting, there would not be blood clotting at the entrance wound. Zach, her time of death was 7 a.m., but the time of the incident was approximately 3:30 a.m.."

"Bingo! Bingo, Rebecca! Thank you!" Zach thanked her, hung up, and shouted, "Gotcha, you arrogant bastard!"

Chapter Fourteen

Russ was arrested at his home that same day at 7:30 p.m. "Russ Jenkins?" the officer asked as he answered his door.

"Yes, that's me. What can I do for you, officer"? Russ responded.

"You're under arrest for the murder of Melodie Jenkins. You have the right…" the officer continued. "You're an idiot, in fact the whole police department is a bunch of morons! I wasn't even in the country when my wife was murdered. You bastards, go find her killer!" Russ shouted as he was taken away in handcuffs.

Jean happened to be at Russ's, thank goodness, so she could look after the kids.

As soon as they arrived at the station, Zach was there to greet Russ.

"Good evening, Mr. Jenkins", Zach extended a warm welcome. "Thanks for coming in this evening, he said sarcastically. We need to revisit your alibi. What time did you say you went to dinner with Melodie? What time did you make love?" Zach continued on with his questions, making sure Russ's story remained consistent.

Russ was clearly annoyed now, but managed to respond with, "Nothing has changed since my first and last statement, Detective Willis."

Zach continued, "Mr. Jenkins, the forensics team completed a rape test kit on Melodie to see if she was sexually assaulted by the intruder and if so, if there was DNA present. Mr. Jenkins, there was none. None at all, Mr. Jenkins," Zach emphasized articulately. He continued, "You told me on our first interview that you 'thanked God you got to make love to your wife before you left for the Bahamas', but you did not. She had no signs of sexual activity at all, Mr. Jenkins. It's one thing for a man to lie about having sex, but what else are you lying about? You're under arrest for your wife's murder, you son of a bitch!" Zach held back the fact that his alibi has been debunked due to the time of attack occurring at about 3:30 a.m., although her time of death was approximately 7:00 a.m.

Russ was in absolute disbelief! He was still grieving! How could they be so stupid! He kept his rage in check, however, maintaining his composure, while assuring the detective they had the wrong guy and in the meantime a savage, cold-hearted killer was on the streets.

"I think it's time I got a lawyer, Detective Willis. This conversation is over." Russ said with a confident, almost cocky tone.

The District Attorney prosecuting Russ, John Heald, won bail of one million dollars based on the violence of the crime and the possibility of Russ fleeing the country. He needed a very, very good lawyer and he knew just whom to call. Kevin Arneson. Kevin was the best defense attorney money can buy in Omaha. He was able to prove innocence in dozens of cases where the community had the defendants convicted before their first day in court.

Kevin was a handsome man in his late thirties. He had perfectly groomed dark hair, with a dark bronze tanning-bed tan and bright white perfect teeth. His dark brown eyes were piercing and convincing. And, he was always dressed to kill, even when he was 'off hours' because, in his mind, and probably rightfully so, every moment in the pubic was an advertisement. Lawyers must be alert, have an insane attention to detail, exude an air of confidence, and come across as your best friend—unless you end up on the opposing side! He was all of this, even when hitting the gym, which he obviously did multiple times a week. Like Russ used to do.

Russ explained his predicament to Kevin. He explained how he somehow got himself into this mess even though he was proven to be in the Bahamas at the time of his wife's murder. His Traveling Executive Assistant was even with him and was a witness to his whereabouts.

Kevin patiently listened to Russ also explain that an intruder had broken into the back foyer door, they never found the gun, and that he's been cooperating with the police this whole time. He hadn't disclosed that his traveling executive assistant was also his lover and had been throughout their whole marriage. That didn't mean he killed his wife; just that he's a schmuck.

Kevin had heard it all before. He'd seen it all before. And he'd fought for it all before. He took on the case, but it wasn't going to be cheap. He needed a half a million-dollar retainer fee, upfront. He assured Russ that he would win the case. The spouse is always the main suspect, and since the prosecution didn't have any other suspects, they were desperate and started reaching for straws to get a conviction and close the case. Without the murder weapon and with his proven alibi, they'd win the case.

"First, Mr. Arneson, get me out of jail!" Russ demanded.

The million-dollar bail would cost Russ one hundred thousand dollars of his hard earned cash. The bond agent would cover the remaining nine hundred thousand with an insurance policy issued to the Court. Win or lose, he might get back a portion of the hundred thousand dollars. He really had no choice, though, since he certainly didn't have an extra million laying around.

Russ was devastated. That's six hundred thousand on just the first day of his arrest! Those bastards have no idea what they are doing to him! And his children! The only way to come up with this kind of money was to get access to Melodie's life insurance policies that Melodie and Russ set up for the kids so many years ago. They had purchased a paid-up insurance policy that would take care of the cost for RJ's special needs. He knew each daughter had a three-million-dollar policy in the event of either parent's death.

Russ was desperate and made the call to Challenge Life from jail. Sandra, the receptionist answered the phone, and after listening to the prerecorded message that plays anytime someone is receiving a call from inside a prison, she accepted the call.

"Thank you for calling Challenge Life. How may I help you today?" she announced in an overly cheerful voice, not at all suspecting it to be Russ on the other end.

"Sandra, my lady. How are you?" he asks.

She whispered with excitement, "Oh my God, Russ! I can't believe they arrested you!"

Sandra always had a great deal of respect for Russ; and perhaps even a little crush. She was a slightly overweight woman in her fifties, who will probably always be a receptionist. She was so good at it; such a pleasant voice, did exactly what was asked of her by her supervisors, never questioned authority, and was very dependable. Russ never missed a morning of greeting her with his big smile and he always had a way of making her feel beautiful, complimenting her outfit, or something she'd done with her hair. He always found something to compliment her. She absolutely loved the attention. And what he didn't know was that every morning when she knew he would be in the office, she would dress up just a little more and put a little more time into her hair and makeup. But she knew, even if he wasn't married to the most beautiful woman in Omaha, that she didn't have a chance with him, but he sure made for a great fantasy for her.

"Yes, things are pretty rough right now. I'm in disbelief too. My children and I are just devastated, and now instead of grieving the loss of my wife, I'm having to fight for my freedom! Who would have ever guessed this, right? Hey, can you get me to Rick? And, you keep that place running, Sandra. They could never do it without you!"

"Sure thing, Russ. And, it's going to be okay. You're an innocent man. They cannot convict an innocent man." She said with confidence.

'Oh yes they can', he thought, as she transferred the call to Rick, the best person he could go to for help in accessing the life insurance funds.

After a similar exchange with Rick as with Sandra, Rick assured Russ he would be able to get him access to his funds through his whole life insurance policy right away. "We have to just complete the form for the loan against your policy and it'll be in your account within several hours."

"Thank you, Rick. I appreciate you." With somewhat of a feeling of relief, he knew he'd be out of jail within the next twenty-four hours and get his high-ticket lawyer paid. But, he needed more money. Six hundred thousand dollars were gone in a blink of an eye. He sure as hell wasn't planning on that. His head was spinning with fear, followed by ideas he later realized were impractical, followed by panic, then new ideas. He knew he had to borrow from the girls' insurance policies, which left a gut wrenching tug in his stomach. But there was simply no other way.

At 4:45 p.m. sharp, Russ heard the sweetest three words. "Jenkins! You're out!" hollered the guard.

Waiting for him was none other than Mr. Kevin Arneson. Oh, how Russ was elated to see him! After quick handshakes, and pleasantries, they agreed to meet first thing in the morning to cover every minute detail of his case. In addition, Russ was instructed to bring his payment for his legal fees.

The adrenaline was pumping as he jumped into his Mercedes to head over to Jean's place. They had to talk. He blasted classical music so he could lose himself in every stroke of the bow on the violins, the humming of the cellos, and the singing of the French horns. Despite his attempts to drown out his fury over how quickly six hundred thousand dollars vanished in a matter of hours, it simply did not work. In fact, his emotional love for this music fueled his emotional love for money, which fueled his fury at its quick disappearance.

Jean knew Russ was a mess right now. So she did what she did best—dressed provocatively and greeted him as a ball of happiness. She didn't expect him to want to make love today, but she simply wanted to give him something to smile about. She knew he was innocent and it would all work out. But right now, she knew he would be worried sick and angry at the world. So, as his mistress, her role was to simply give him something to be happy about. Of course, her expectation was also that she would soon become the wife rather than the mistress. But for now, she would continue to play her part.

When he walked in the door, she was in her black yoga pants and hot pink sports bra, stretching on a yoga mat along with the yoga instructor on the TV, Lynn Paula. She purposely let her hair lose, instead of tying it in a ponytail. It was worth being in her way during some stretches to be sure to take Russ's breath away when he saw her.

Jean sprang to her feet to greet him and gave him a big kiss and an even bigger hug. "There's my Knight in Shining Armor! God, I've missed you! I am so sorry that you had to spend two days in that hell hole. Tonight, it's just you and me, baby. I want to just go back to how it was before, even if only for one night, when we didn't have a care in the world, talked about everything, and laughed at anything", she said as she kept back tears. She wanted to be light and fun for him.

"I've missed you, too, more than you know. Yes, jail does suck, I can tell you that and for the price I'm paying Arneson, I'd best never spend one more hour in that hell hole!" he assured her.

"Jean," he continued, "we need to talk about something for a moment."

"Russ, whatever you need. What can I do to help?"

"Listen, Jean, my bail cost me one hundred thousand dollars and my lawyer is charging half a million dollars—all up front. I need you to put away the credit cards for now. I am not in a position to continue paying those, too. I have to figure this out. I have to figure this out…" he repeated, fading off as if talking to himself.

"Oh, of course, Russ. I understand. I will only use the card for bare necessities from today forward" she agreed, but was afraid to tell him she'd already had fun with it to the tune of ten thousand dollars this month. And, how do we actually define 'bare necessities'? She did need a new purse for spring.

As intended, Jean kept the rest of the night light with silly stories about people she saw out shopping, funny things she saw on TV, and constant flirting. Russ tried to be responsive but he was clearly somewhere else, in his mind. But to her surprise, their evening ended with making love. He was clearly distracted and not relaxed and into it like he usually was, but given the circumstances, she understood. He lay in bed with her for just a few minutes and those few minutes brought him back to the moments at Creighton when they would make amazingly wild love and then just hold each other, not talking, just listening to each others' heartbeats. How he missed that simplicity. But, for now, he had to get up, get dressed and meet his blood sucking attorney. Damn, he had better be as good as they say he is!

After a trip to the bank, Russ met with Kevin Arneson as planned. Arneson had already spoken with the prosecutor and knew this would be a tough case. Sure, Russ was in the Bahamas at the time of Melodie's actual death, with his suspected lover no less, but based on the theory of the pathologist, Melodie was shot much earlier and simply did not die until he was in the Bahamas. He didn't have much to go on, but he had to build a defense to provide the defendant with a fair trial and to justify the half a mil he had just made. The intruder theory and reasonable doubt was really all he had. Not having a murder weapon greatly enhanced the probability of getting to reasonable doubt.

Russ explained his story again, and again. He did come clean about Jean being his lover, but according to Russ, that relationship just started after she was hired as his Traveling Executive Assistant. He didn't think anyone needed to know that their affair started up after only six months of marriage to Melodie. No one needs to know that.

After his meeting with Arneson, it was off to Challenge Life. His welcome was warm by many, especially Sandra who threw her arms around him with a big hug. For a few, it was lukewarm to cool, leading him to only imagine the water-cooler discussions. It took about fifteen minutes for him to make his way from the front door to his office, at which time he booted up his computer and went to his file containing all of their life insurance policies He and Melodie planned well for the kids. They each had three million dollar whole life policies with cash values of one million dollars each. Those funds could be borrowed at a moment's notice with no questions asked.

First he brought up Ashley's account. Of the three million dollars in her policy, it had one million in cash value. He started completing the form to borrow the million dollars and needed to indicate the account number where the money would go. As he looked at his family picture on the desk, he rocked back and forth, thinking, contemplating, evaluating. Which account? Which account should he use? He opened up his file cabinet and pulled the manila file folder labeled "Misc." and found the post-it note where his Bahamas bank account number was jotted down. He carefully entered the number, making sure it was accurate, paused, and hit 'submit'.

Next, Kim's account. They were all opened at the same time with the same values. Therefore, he knew one million dollars of cash value would also be available. Repeating the process, he borrowed the one million from her account too.

Then, Beth's account. Repeat.

In a matter of minutes, he had another three million dollars. Stolen from his daughters' life insurance policies. He knew he would replace the money at some point, though. Once he got through this ordeal, he'd pay the policies back to ensure the girls had their full en-titlements. Although, he knew he just had to do what he had to do right now, this made his heart hurt. He's done his fair share of shoddy business dealings to make a buck, but to steal from his kids? This hurt him, but he'd pay it back. He was sure of it.

Thinking of his kids, he missed them terribly over the past few days and he could only imagine how devastating it was for them to have lost their mother to a senseless murder and then have their father put in jail on suspicion of doing such a heinous act. He made a quick call to the Farnsworths to arrange to pick up the kids and take them home. Charles and Elizabeth convinced Russ to come over for a visit with the kids but said that taking them home would not be such a good idea. They were probably correct when they painted a picture of lawyers, detectives, news crews and God knows who else knock-ing on his door round the clock. This just wouldn't provide for a safe and stable environment for the kids right now. So, he agreed to a visit at their place that evening. God, he needed their hugs to-night. But, the hugs were distant, and kind of cold. They spoke of the teasing they got from the kids at school. They asked so many questions about why the cops would arrest him for killing their mother; so many questions he could not answer. All he could do was assure them they would find the right guy and this would all be over. Russ hugged Beth goodbye as she sobbed that she wanted her mommy back and her daddy. He wished he could make her wishes come true. He wanted, more than anything, to get the family reunited at their own home and get back to normal, and watch them play their sports, hang out with their friends, and live normal lives.

As Russ arrived at his home, he was greeted by Katie Trumanski of News Channel 8. He faked a smile and plowed his way past her, and into his home, ignoring every question. He opened his front door as quickly as he could to avoid the news shark and three additional news crews' cards fell from the door jam.

Finally, he poured a shot of Hennessy Cognac on the rocks. It had never tasted so good. As he sipped his drink, he started thinking about Jean, but resisted the temptation to have her come over. That would just look bad right now. And after spending a couple nights in jail, he would sleep hard in his own bed tonight.

Chapter Fifteen

This case was one that kept Zach up at night. He knew he had the right suspect, but everything was circumstantial. Russ was guilty. He was guilty as sin. How could a father kill his children's mother? As a father himself, Zach just couldn't get past this and it was affecting his sleep. He had to have an iron-clad case against him to get justice for Melodie, Melodie's parents, and most importantly, the kids. The scene was clearly staged to look like an intruder. A classic error that novice criminals make out of haste is breaking the glass from the inside, throwing shards of glass outside. The blood clotting at the entrance wound hours before actual death blew a major hole in his alibi. And how close was Jean to Russ anyway? He'd interviewed Jean a few times already and she never admitted to having an affair with Russ, but she was certainly nervous and agitated. There must be more to them.

Joe was already on it. He suspected the two of having an affair from the get-go, as did Zach. The difference was that Joe lived for stakeouts, so he'd been watching Russ's moves from day one. Joe has followed him to Jean's condo on a few occasions but they were always good. They were really good. Never has Joe seen them together except at the funeral. Joe watched as Russ arrived, knocked, Jean answered the door and let him in. He was there for forty-five minutes to a few hours. He left. At no time did he witness them kissing at the door, going on a date, nothing.

Until today. Something odd happened today. When Russ left the county jail, he arrived at Jean's. Nothing out of the ordinary—he still didn't witness them together. But this time, he unlocked her door with a key he already had in his possession. He didn't knock this time. Nor was the door left unlocked where he could simply walk in and announce his presence cautiously, as if he were a co-worker coming in and announcing his arrival. No, this time it was evident that Russ Jenkins had a key to Jean Cameron's condo. There was no work circumstance that could explain that. "Zach is going to eat this up", Joe said under his breath to himself. Joe's guess was that Jean and Russ were in this together. They killed Melodie so they could live their own lives together.

When Joe provided this information to Zach, he was intrigued but not overwhelmingly enthusiastic as he thought he would be.

"Joe, as always, good work. This is great information. However, maybe he got a key after Melodie's death? Maybe Jean has been there to console his grieving heart for the past six months, and then it turned into an affair. We need more. We need proof as to if there was an affair prior to the murder, and so far, they have checked out." Zach knew Joe was right, but what was happening now was not nearly as incriminating as finding out what was going on while Melodie was still alive.

"Zach," Joe went on, "remember the day of Melodie's murder when he went to check into his hotel and they handed him a key upon arrival, as if the hotel agent knew Russ? As if, perhaps he was a 'regular'? Well, why would he be a regular at a hotel in his hometown? Maybe they have video surveillance to see if anyone, particularly Jean, joined him at that hotel."

"Let's go see the hotel staff at the Holiday Inn Express, Joe!"

The hotel confirmed their suspicions. Not only were they able to pick Jean out of a lineup as the 'woman who met Russ in the hotel', but they also confirmed that she met Russ there on a regular basis, including the day on which Melodie was murdered.

Zach brought this information to Mr. Heald and they were beginning to build a strong circumstantial case against Russ Jenkins. But it was still just circumstantial. It's hard to win juries over without hard scientific evidence, thanks to TV crime shows. Juries want to see the smoking gun these days. But without the smoking gun, they were going to have to look deeper into the marriage and finances of Russ and Melodie, and when exactly Jean entered the picture. The needed to conduct a new search of the Jenkins residence, along with the hotel room Russ checked into the night of the murder. Although, six months later, the investigators did not have their hopes up.

The hotel staff let the investigators into room 321, the room Russ checked into the night of the murder. They hadn't seen Russ since, which was fairly odd considering that they saw him two or three times a week when he was in town, or at least every other week when he was traveling out of the state. But, it was all over the news that Mrs. Jenkins had been murdered, so it didn't seem all that odd that he'd changed his daily habits in light of such tragic circumstances. Since they hadn't seen him, they hadn't been able to return the duffel bag to him that he'd left in room 321. The duffel bag was empty so it didn't seem to be a priority to return it to him, and they'd forgotten. But it had been sitting on the lost and found shelf all this time. They turned it over to the police who immediately sent it for processing, hoping to find some kind of forensic evidence to tie it to the murder scene. They were actually hoping the gun would be stashed inside a pocket somewhere, but they didn't get that lucky. Still no murder weapon.

Something else was on Zach's mind that had been bugging him for some time. Russ was in the Bahamas to meet with a client. Who was this client? Did they actually meet? Could this client shed some light on Russ's alibi, state of mind, or anything else incriminating? He needed to have a conversation with his new friends at Challenge Life. They ought to have records of Russ's meetings.

Chapter Sixteen

Russ slept surprisingly well, considering the stress he'd been under. The combination of cognac with a little sleep aide sure did the trick. His phone rang early that morning, he didn't even have a chance to finish blending his usual smoothie of almond milk, bananas and strawberries.

"Mr. Jenkins? Good morning. I'm Sean Shafter, of Shafter and Sons. I am sorry for calling so early; I hope I didn't wake you. I'm sorry for your loss and my condolences to you and your family. I was hired by Jeffrey Maltzer, your estate attorney, to manage your children's assets. My objective is to look out for the welfare of your children's estates, which will allow you to spend your time focusing on your other important matters without the extra worry of your children," he explained.

Russ's mind was racing, his heart was pounding like mad, and he immediately started sweating. 'Could this really be happening to me?' he thought to himself. The day after he borrowed from his kids' life insurance policies, their estate attorney calls! He realized that the money probably wasn't transferred just yet, hopefully. Maybe he could delay it! Russ was great at appearing calm and charismatic, even during times of great stress, so he eagerly thanked Mr. Shafter for his assistance. To buy himself some time, he told Mr. Shafter that he'd provide the account numbers later, that they were at the office. However, Mr. Shafter replied, "Oh, not necessary, Mr. Jenkins. I have them right here. I've got what I need; I'm simply giving you a courtesy call."

Russ thanked him, hung up, and began to panic. He paced the kitchen, then sat down at the table, almost in a daze, then paced again. Thinking. Thinking. Leaving the half-blended smoothie, he brushed his teeth, put on deodorant, threw a little gel in his hair to make it look presentable and changed into his pressed Hudson boot -cut jeans and blue and white striped Polo shirt. He grabbed his black belt and black polished shoes, threw them on while running out the door and headed straight to Challenge Life. He had to see if he could stop those transfers. On his way, racing to the office, he realized that it was perfectly legal for him to borrow money from the whole life policies. That's why they got whole life policies instead of term life. But the account he had transferred them into could come into question.

"Russ! What are you doing here? I thought you were taking some time off. How are you doing? Is there anything we can do for you?" was the common sentiment he heard as he hurried to his office, to his computer. Trying to be as inconspicuous as possible, he calmly smiled and thanked those who offered to help and offered condolences, and made it to his office.

He poked at the keyboard, too quickly, making too many typos and errors. With a deep breath, he relaxed and tried logging in again. Finally, he was in.

Transfer Processing $1,000,000

Transfer Processing $1,000,000

Transfer Processing $1,000,000

All three were processing, which meant they could not be stopped, but it also meant that the money was still in the life accounts. Only people logged into the money management system for Challenge Life would see the transfers; whereas if Shafter logged into the girls' actual accounts now, it would show all of the money still there in the account balances.

"Good morning." Russ heard a familiar voice at the front desk and knew immediately who it was.

"I am Detective Zach Willis. I'm here to see Mr. Barnes, please."

During his short five-minute wait, Sandra chatted with him, talking about the weather and other niceties. She had a feeling it was regarding Russ, so she also was quite anxious, but that didn't come through—at least Zach didn't notice.

Zach asked Mr. Barnes who would have a record of Russ's clients and meetings. In particular, he needed to know the name and contact information for the client Russ was meeting in the Bahamas. Mr. Barnes knew of a client Russ had worked with for years in the Bahamas but did not know his name. He asked Sandra to pull up Russ's meetings, but she apologetically informed Mr. Barnes and Detective Willis that she hadn't kept his schedule, especially since

Ms. Cameron became his Executive Assistant. Mr. Barnes referred Detective Willis to Jean Cameron. He was certain she would know because she met the client with Russ.

It was still early enough in the day, so Zach was hopeful he'd catch Jean still home before she left to do, well, whatever it was she did now that she's taking time off work, too.

As soon as the front double glass doors were closing behind Zach, Russ made a quick call. "Good morning, Jean. Hey, I have to speak softly. I'm at the office and Zach Willis just stopped by. He's on his way to see you. He wants to know who we met in the Bahamas the day Melodie was murdered," he explained.

"Russ, that was the appointment that you set up, so I don't know who that client was. And, he stood us up, and we had to leave quickly for the airport", she reminded him.

"Right. So, neither you nor the client would really be of any help to Detective Willis. But I just wanted to give you a heads up that he's coming over."

"I just got out of the shower and I'm dripping wet, or I'd run out the door before he gets here!"

"Oooh, stay like that until I get there this afternoon," Russ teased. She still loves it when he flirts with her. It had been over twenty-two years and it still made her giddy.

Jean barely had time to dry her hair, put on some clothes and had just started to put on her makeup when she heard the knock at the door. She didn't invite the detective in, but she fully cooperated while they stood together at the front door.

"We were supposed to meet with Russ's client at 9 a.m. We waited in the restaurant where we were meeting, but he never showed. Russ was about to call him to see if he was on his way when he got the tragic call from Glaucia." Jean was proud of her memory of the details and she had a sense of confidence about her that Zach picked up on. She was very matter of fact and professional.

"Thank you, Miss Cameron. Could you please provide me with the client's name and contact information?"

"I don't have it here with me. It would be at the office. The company will have it," she assured him.

"Actually, they don't. Sandra and Mr. Barnes said you would have it because you schedule his meetings, especially overseas clients. Is that not correct, Miss Cameron?" he probed with somewhat of a condescending tone.

"I don't schedule all of them, Detective Willis. Russ always schedules the ones with certain high profile clients. They are very high dollar clients, so he likes to manage those directly," she explained.

"Oh, I see. Thank you. One last question, Miss Cameron. When would you say that you and Mr. Jenkins started having an intimate relationship?"

"How dare you, Detective! I'm a professional at my place of employment". She was furious and more than anything, scared to death. How did she end up in this situation? How did she end up with a life-long lover who is accused of killing his wife? And even worse, she was with him the day of the murder. How can they consider Russ a suspect when it was proven he was in the Bahamas? She didn't sign up for this mess and she was terrified. She was scared for herself and she was scared she'd say the wrong thing and hurt Russ.

"Forgive me. Thank you for your time, Miss Cameron. Please call me if you think of any details, no matter how small, that might help us put away the monster who did this to Mrs. Jenkins. We need to protect the community," he added as he nodded. He really wasn't expecting an answer to his last question; he simply wanted to see how she would respond to it.

Chapter Seventeen

Sean quickly got to work to oversee the life insurance policies. The paperwork showed that each Jenkins daughter had a three-million-dollar policy in the event of the death of one of their parents. After carefully reviewing the policies, ensuring he understood all the legal facets, he logged into the account, with the information provided by Jeffrey Maltzer. Ashley's, Kimberly's, and Beth's accounts all had one million dollars transferred from them with today's date. "What the hell?" he said out loud, although no one was around to hear him or even attempt to answer the question. "I'll be damned."

"Maltzer, Shafter here. I found something of interest. Six hundred thousand was withdrawn four days ago and three million was transferred out today from the three daughters' life insurance accounts. Do you know anything about that?"

"You're kidding, right?" Malzter responded, genuinely assuming Shafter was trying to get a rise out of him. After realizing he was being dead serious, Maltzer knew it was time to bring in the financial expert—Mr. Ronald Caswell. He was the best forensic accountant in the city, if not in the state. Hell, maybe even the best in the nation. Caswell has been Maltzer's go-to guy for his toughest cases for the past twenty-five years.

Standing only five foot, seven inches tall, with a generously round stature, thick lensed glasses outlined with heavy black frames and graying light brown hair, Ron typically went unnoticed. He had a vast array of brown slacks that pretty much all looked the same, and blue striped or checkered short sleeve button-down shirts. Once in a while he would go out on a limb and pair a green striped shirt with his brown pants. While he should have worn a white undershirt all the time, sometimes he did and sometimes he didn't. Interestingly, however, as much of a non-fashion guru that Ron was, you would only find the best of watches on his wrist. Never Rolex, though. Rolex draws too much attention and comes across as an 'attention seeker' brand. Not Ron. Ron liked to stay under the radar, unnoticed, yet he valued a good precise watch more than any other physical possession. His go-to watch was a Patek Philippe, passed down to him through generations starting with his great grandfather, valued by today's standards, at roughly seventeen thousand dollars. By now, the simple crystal face was scratched all to hell and the band looked worn, but that damn watch was never off, ever, by even a second.

Ron was always a numbers guy; in fact, he was a numbers kid. Math came easy to him and he couldn't understand how other students didn't just 'get it' whatever 'it' was in math. So, it was no surprise that he pursued a degree and career in accounting. During his time at Harvard, another accounting student, Julie, took an interest in Ron. He wasn't used to that kind of attention as he spent his whole life as an introvert and not much of a lady's man. She was also in accounting and they both graduated from Harvard and married shortly after. He loved Julie, but mostly simply because she loved him. She saw through the thick glasses and his pudgy figure and saw how brilliant he was and she was confident he would provide a comfortable life style for both of them. Neither really wanted children, so they could focus on their careers.

Ron landed a high paying corporate accounting job with a fortune 100 company while Julie found an accounting position with a small start-up company. After six years of marriage, Ron was pulling in two hundred and fifty thousand a year plus incredible perks. Julie was spending his money as fast as he could make it. She then found herself to be pregnant and when Ron found out the baby was not his, but rather the owner of the small accounting firm where she worked, he immediately filed for divorce. That's when he learned how much money she was siphoning out of the marriage from his income and also learned she was making twice the amount she disclosed to him. After being raked over the coals, Ron left corporate accounting and became a forensic accountant, focusing on divorce cases only.

He knew all the tricks, and he was on a mission to save every man from the Julies of the world. To his disappointment, however, he learned that most of the time, it was the Julies he was saving from the Johns of the world. Nonetheless, he was damn good at it and the first one to be called upon. Fortunately, Maltzer and Caswell became quite the duo after their first case together so Caswell was on Maltzer's speed dial and would take on any of his cases he could possibly squeeze in. Ron never did remarry.

Zach grabbed a cup of coffee from Starbucks. Yes, that was how he ordered it, "Large black coffee, please." He was not going to fall for the trendy 'Starbucks vocabulary' no matter how much it made him sound like an outsider in the place. He grabbed his coffee and went back to his Honda. Recalling his quick interview with Jean, he sat deeply in thought. Why would no one in his company, especially Russ's Traveling Executive Assistant, know who Russ flew to the Bahamas to meet? He was supposedly such a high-ticket client. Why didn't anyone know who the clients are in the Bahamas or Bermuda? He needed to find out who he was scheduled to meet with. So far, besides the initial interview immediately following the murder, the kids have not been interviewed. They were only asked where they were at the time of the murder and they all said at their grandparents. But, now it was time to interview the kids to find out if they knew just a little bit more than what they were telling.

Zach lined up a time to speak with each of the kids, briefly, through Shafter. Prior to bringing in the girls, Shafter told Zach his findings regarding the missing millions from the girls' life insurance policies. "I've got Caswell on it so once he discovers where the money went, I'll be back in touch."

By this time, six months after the murder, RJ had completely crumbled. He was unable to go to school and was spending much of his time at a facility to serve people with special needs. He had become non-functional and the Farnsworths just did not know what else to do. They prayed for guidance and Melodie's forgiveness for making RJ get this extra help that he did not want. It devastated them, but he needed help far beyond the capabilities of his grandparents. Melodie was RJ's rock and gave him the drive to succeed.

Zach interviewed Ashley, Kimberly and Beth separately, with Shafter present. He simply asked, "Your dad traveled quite a bit to other places. Do you know any of the clients' names he went to visit when he traveled?"

Beth said she knew he mentioned a client by the name of Philip Moore. She particularly remembered that name because she had a boy in her class name Phil and his last name was Morris. So, she thought it was funny when her dad said he was going to meet with Philip Moore. The other two girls had no recollection of any clients' names, but they also rarely paid any attention to what their dad was saying anyway, unless it was something fun that pertained to them.

"Philip Moore, Miss Sandra", Zach repeated when he called Challenge Life to find more information about this client.

"Detective Willis, I'm sorry, but I'm not showing any client in our database by the name of Philip Moore. Are you sure you have the name correct?" Sandra responded. She provided Zach additional names of other clients in the Bahamas and Bermuda and perhaps one of those clients was who Russ was scheduled to meet the morning of Melodie's murder. Zach spent the rest of the afternoon trying to contact each of the names provided by Challenge Life. One of them confirmed he hadn't done business with Challenge Life in three years; another one was dead; another confirmed she did business with Challenge Life and had her accounts with them, but her agent was not Russ and she meets with her agent when she goes back to visit her family in Omaha. That left one more possible client, Pete Mobley. So far he had not gotten a return call from him, but perhaps Beth mistook "Pete Mobley" for "Philip Moore". They sure didn't sound very much alike, but they did have the same initials.

Chapter Eighteen

While Zach was trying to figure out who Russ and Jean met in the Bahamas, Ron was busy digging into the finances of the Jenkins, uncovering some interesting anomalies. In so doing, he tracked Russ's expenses while traveling and discovered a handful of charges to the Daiquiri Shack. On learning this, Zach thought there were enough expenses there that it seemed he may be a regular when he was out that way, and some of the employees may actually know him. Now seemed like a better time than ever to make a trip to the Bahamas. Unlike Mr. Jenkins, Zach didn't have a corporate G4 to fly to the Bahamas, so he booked on the next flight out and paid the hefty price of eight hundred and fifty-five dollars. Coach seat. Middle. Doesn't get much worse than that. But, about six hours later, he touched down in the Bahamas.

It didn't take long for Zach to realize the appeal of this place. The laid back culture, the music, the freedom and the beauty—of the land

and the women—could be addicting. A local cabbie, originally from New York, but who visited the Bahamas once on vacation and never went back, took Zach to the Daiquiri Shack. Zach made himself comfortable and ordered himself the famous Gully Wallup.

"Gully Wallup?" the bartender chuckled. "You've got to be a tourist! It's a Gully Wash and I'll make one extra special good for you. What brings you to the Bahamas?" she managed to ask with a smile despite the fact that she'd asked the same question all night long for ten long years. But, she loved it. She loved the people and she loved their gossip.

"Oh, how embarrassing! Yes, guilty as charged; I'm a tourist!" Zach laughed. "Along with probably everyone else around here. I'd like a Gully Wash and an ice water, please."

After making some small talk, shooting the breeze about what got this nice bartender to the Bahamas in the first place, and where 'home' was for her, and other topics she discussed hundreds of times a week, Zach took out a picture of Russ.

"So, I'm trying to reconnect with an old friend of mine. Have you seen him here at all?" he asked.

The bubbly bartender took a quick look and responded that she hadn't. She then asked to see it again and had a change of heart. "I think that might be the guy who travels here every now and then. He looks like the guy who always asks for Sara. She'll be coming in in about an hour if you want to check with her," she told him.

The Gully Wash was definitely not what it was cracked up to be. Zach didn't think he could choke down another one of those sweet drinks, so he ordered a vodka and water and sipped on that and his glass of ice water while he waited for Sara to come in. He and the bartender continued to chit chat between other conversations with other patrons, but this girl clearly knew nothing about Russ.

Sara arrived right on time and the bubbly bartender didn't wait a second to send her to Zach to show her the picture.

"Is that the guy who always asks for you when he's in town?"

"Oh, yes, that's Russ! Is he in town now? How do you know him?" she asked Zach enthusiastically.

"Oh, good! I'm so glad you know him, Sara. I just know that he visits here every now and then and was hoping to catch him. It would also be nice to catch up with Philip Moore. Do you know him, too?" Zach asked Sara, while trying not to notice her deep unlined Bahama tan.

"Fillip Moore, the bartender?" she asked with surprise. Neither Zach nor Russ seemed the type to be friends with the bartender at the Tiki Bar where she worked prior to coming to the Daiquiri Shack.

"Yes, yes, of course, Fillip Moore the bartender. Russ once told me if I ever end up in the Bahamas to make sure I visit his bar because he always takes great care of him. Does he work at your bar?"

She informed him that the last she knew, he worked at the Tiki Bar at the hotel where Russ usually stayed and that his last name wasn't really 'Moore' but that's what people call him because his real last name was very long and hard to pronounce.

Zach wanted to scream, 'I've got you, you bastard!' He had done this for so long that these types of twists and turns didn't throw him off on the outside, but deep down inside, they made him reel just like they did from the beginning of his first case. He couldn't jump to conclusions, though; he was still waiting on a call from Pete Mobley to see if he was the client Russ was scheduled to meet with on that deadly morning.

After finishing his drink, he headed over to the Tiki Bar at Russ's regular hotel to see if he might be lucky enough to meet the famous Philip Moore-whatever. During his cab ride over, he got a call from Mr. Mobley.

"No, Detective Willis, I have not met with Mr. Jenkins in at least a year. He does a great job; he's a brilliant financial agent, but I just haven't been in a position to take my finances further for some time."

So, none of the four clients on Challenge Life's books were Russ's clients; nor had any of them had a meeting scheduled with him the morning of Melodie's death.

'Oh, how I can't wait to meet Philip Moore the bartender!' he said to himself.

"Hello! Welcome to the Ocean's Tiki Bar. What are you in the mood for?" the young twenty-something bartender wearing a tag that read 'Emmanuel' asked?

"Anything but a Gully Wash, my man, Emmanuel!" Zach said with a laugh. "Is Fillip working tonight?" he asked his Haitian bartender. He couldn't help but notice that everyone who lived in the Bahamas, regardless of where they came from, was in great shape and was attractive.

Emmanuel said that Fillip was off tonight but would be in tomorrow for the afternoon shift. With that information, Zach was lucky that the hotel had a couple of rooms available. He checked in and made himself at home. He hated being away from home and was glad it was infrequent. He called his wife, and told her and his kids about what life seemed to be like in the Bahamas. He promised to take them all there sometime for vacation. With that, it was time for lights out with the windows open. He felt the cool breeze and the fresh smells and sounds, which put him to sleep like a baby.

He enjoyed sleeping in and went for a long walk along the beach, although he surely didn't bring appropriate Bahamas clothes. He was sure to hit the Ocean's Tiki Bar at one o'clock for lunch and just as promised, a bartender wearing a name tag with 'Fillip' greeted him as if he really did want to be there. Everyone seems to love his job here in the Bahamas!

"Hello, my friend!" Fillip said. "What can I get you? Having lunch with us today?"

Zach requested a plain iced tea, unsweetened, and fish tacos. "So, Fillip," he continued, your friend, Sara, said I may find you here." He showed Fillip the picture of Russ and asked if he knew him.

Fillip definitely remembered him for a couple reasons. For one, he was an irregular regular. He was only there every few months, but when he was in town, he was there every night, all night—at least until Sara went to the Daiquiri Shack. Now, when he's in town, he starts off at the Tiki Bar since it is in the hotel property, then he leaves, presumably to go see Sara.

Zach confirmed with Fillip that he had no business dealings with Russ. At twenty-two years old, no wife, girlfriend or kids, he wasn't anywhere near ready to start talking life insurance.

"Fillip, I'm a detective from Omaha, Nebraska and Mr. Russ

Jenkins has been charged with murdering his wife. His alibi was that he was here in the Bahamas at the time of the murder to meet with you, although he spelled the name "Philip. I'm going to need you to testify, my friend", Zach explained.

"You're kidding me, right? Oh my God, I can hardly believe that! Sara, oh my God, Sara has spent a lot of time with this jackass. I think they had a thing going. Thank God he didn't hurt her. Does she know what you just told me? Why the hell would he say he was meeting me?" Fillip asked one question after another, leaving no time for Zach to answer any of them. All the better. Zach didn't want to answer any of them. He knew Fillip was just processing. But then he asked again, "Detective, why would Russ say he was meeting me? I'm a bartender! Why the hell would he involve me?"

Zach answered this one to the best of his ability. "Fillip, I think he simply used your name to make up a fictitious client. He knew you as Fillip with an "F" and when he needed to create a fictitious name, he thought of Phillip. You're known by your friends and clients by a portion of your last name, 'Moore', which created the perfect fake name for Mr. Jenkins. He's been using your name for some time as an excuse to come to the Bahamas. I need you to testify that you did not have a meeting scheduled with him the morning of his wife's murder."

As soon as Zach left the Tiki Bar, Fillip called Sara. "Oh my God, Sara, you're not going to believe this….."

What Zach could not explain was why the secretive visits to the Bahamas? What was he doing here if he wasn't meeting clients?

His answer came soon enough.

"Willis. Shafter here."

"Yes, what's up?" Zach asked with a new found eagerness.

"The forensic accountant I told you about, Ronald Caswell, came up with some very interesting details into the Jenkins' financials. He wants to meet with us. He wants to meet with us now, Zach." Shafter urged.

"I'm leaving Nassau tonight. Let's meet at your office tomorrow morning at 9:30 a.m.".

Chapter Nineteen

Zach beat Ron to Shafter's office. Oh how Zach hated Sean's office. For one, it was on the third floor of the building in which the homicide department is situated and there was no working elevator. And, Sean's office was perfectly organized, making everyone else who has a desk in this world feel disorderly and unorganized. One would think Sean didn't even work. He was a bit OCD, though, so he worked hard and always puts things back in their place or created a file immediately. He also had a great big conference table in his office so there was room to spread out, which would probably be necessary when Ron dove in to show them his findings. They were each enjoying a cup of coffee, as Sean began to tell Zach more about Ron. He was defending him by discussing his brilliance before Zach had ever even met him.

Ron made it. He was five minutes late because of the stairs. He was out of breath, but he made it. But not all the files did.

"S-s-s-ean. Could y-y-you help me pick up some f-f-files that fell on the s-s-stairs?" Ron stuttered slightly as he asked for help. Before he could get his box of files to the table, they scattered to the floor as Ron tried to grasp them. He was too late. Files flew everywhere as Ron let out a firm, "dammit"!

"Ron, goodness! Sit down, catch your breath and I'll go grab the files." Sean assured him. Zach shook Ron's sweaty hand and began picking up the files from the floor as Sean went to retrieve any files in the stairwell.

Zach scooped up the files, gently tossed them on the conference table and excused himself to see if Sean needed help. Finding him halfway to the stairwell, Zach simply asked, "Seriously, Sean?"

Sean smiled and even let out a soft chuckle, "Zach, you're going to love this guy."

"You had better be right."

Ron only had a slight stutter, especially during high stress situations. He'd caught his breath but was sweating through his blue striped shirt. This time he was not wearing an undershirt as he should have been. He had re-sorted the files, which was easy for him because all the papers were clipped into the file folders, so the individual papers stayed intact.

"Let's try this a-a-agin. I'm Ronald Caswell, Sean's forensic accountant. I l-like to make grand entrances!"

With that, the three of them laughed and they agreed Ron did a great job of that this morning. Now, it was time to get down to business.

"Let's start with the l-little stuff, shall we? Mr. Jenkins has made s-s-several stops to the ATM for two hundred or three hundred dollars over the course of some time. Nothing unusual there except that he has made those ATM stops for six years and up to three and four times per week. There's no record of where that money went. So, he's pulled over a million dollars from the joint accounts via ATM, yet joint purchases were not made with the monies", Ron began.

"In addition", Ron continued smoothly, now that he'd recovered from the three floor hike up the stairs and the embarrassment of the morning, "Mr. Jenkins had purchased annuities through Challenge Life. He purchased these annuities with the commissions he has earned at the company. The annuities are for ten to twenty years, meaning the income would not have shown up on his income taxes for many years to come. I need to do a little more digging, but it appears the accounts are located in the Bahamas and Bermuda."

Zach interjected, "This sounds like he's been planning to leave Melodie for some time and was stashing away cash in preparation. Where's the money from the kids' life insurance policies?"

"It appears Mr. Jenkins' defense attorney doesn't have a lot of faith in his client's innocence because Mr. Arneson required half a mil up front! That's some fee! Hey, Shafter, what about it? I've been working for you too cheaply!" Ron joked, although also hoping to hint that perhaps he could get away with charging a little bit more. Shafter, Willis and Caswell all laughed a quick response and got back to business.

"Another hundred thousand went to bail Jenkins out of jail. He had a million-dollar bail so he had to cover ten percent of that in cash to get out. So that is the point six of the missing three point six."

Ron could not yet say where all the ATM purchases went and needed to verify the account information on the accounts in the Bahamas and Bermuda. Zach planned to do a little questioning of Miss Jean Cameron to see if she knew anything about the finances since Russ relied on her for some of his business dealings, while Ron got back to work looking deeper into the entire financial picture of the Jenkins'.

It had been a long day and Zach's head was spinning. A strong case was coming together against Jenkins. Between the time of death versus the time of assault revelation, the glass shards outside the home instead of inside, Zach's Bahamas client being fictitious and actually a young bartender, and millions of dollars missing, a circumstantial case was brewing. But that was the problem—it was all circumstantial. No murder weapon; no witnesses; no confession. But the case was building.

There was one thing that would surely make a great end to his long day, and make him the hero in his home—ice cream! Zach stopped for a tray full of dishes of ice cream—butter pecan for him, chocolate chip for his girls, and strawberry shortcake for his wife. How he loved them and couldn't wait to see the smiles on their faces and smell their hair with each hug. He insisted on hugs and kisses with every departure and every homecoming because he had seen too much pain the world. Hugs and kisses every day were not only priceless, but absolutely essential to his well-being.

The next morning, the first order of business was a visit to Miss Cameron. She wasn't at her condo when he arrived so he called her on the number she had provided him previously. There was no answer, so he slid his card under the door of her condo and left a voice message asking her to contact him at her earliest convenience. He kept it low-key, not to alarm her, and just said he needed to clear up a couple more details. While Zach was certain Russ had killed his wife, he could not ignore the possibility that Jean was either in on the plan, or at least had additional information which could help him.

Jean was able to pick up the call at the time but screened it. She listened to the message and found out it was Mr. Zach Willis…again.

"Russ, what is going on? Why does he keep calling me? I'm scared to death!" Jean said in a panic to Russ. He saw the look of fear in her eyes. Or was it doubt? He wasn't sure. Did she actually think he killed his wife?

Jean wasn't finished, "They keep asking me about our trip to the Bahamas; who we were supposed to meet, and Russ, I don't know! You don't tell me anything about your international clients. I don't know what to say to any of their questions, Russ. I'm scared. I'm scared to death." She trailed off with more tears as Russ held her tight, just assuring her it was going to be okay, and to cooperate but keep their affair off the radar. But she was not quite so sure. She didn't think Russ was capable of killing his wife, but she wasn't so sure that the deck wasn't stacked against him regardless.

Jean left Russ's after lunch and felt compelled to return Zach's call. She was terrified and had butterflies in her stomach, but not cooperating would be even worse. Again, how the hell did she get herself involved in this mess! She asked herself that question every day, multiple times a day.

"Detective. Willis? This is Jean . You called?" she barely exhaled.

Zach arrived at her condo within twenty-two minutes. He asked her about her involvement with Russ's finances. She denied any knowledge and involvement, but Zach had been around too long and her shifty eyes and hesitant responses gave her away. He knew she knew more; and he knew from her body language that she was particularly nervous about it. So, he went for the jugular.

"Miss Cameron, it's time we quit playing games where I ask you questions, pretending that I don't already know that you know the answers, and you pretend you know nothing. You do realize that your boyfriend is charged with murdering his wife, and that you are his mistress? That doesn't look good for you, and my investigative team is finalizing their findings to present to the DA, which would result in your arrest as an accomplice to murder. Now, Miss Cameron, you were either directly involved with Melodie's murder so that you and Russ could live happily ever after, or you know more than you're telling me!"

Before Zach could continue with additional invented material to get Jean to talk, it worked. The flood gates opened and Jean told him exactly what he needed to know, and far more than he expected.

"No! No! Detective, I had nothing, absolutely nothing to do with Melodie's murder! And neither did Russ! We were in the Bahamas together to meet a client. Russ could not have killed Melodie! He just couldn't! I know him! Russ and I have never really been apart. After college he married Melodie, but he and I just couldn't stay away from one another. We tried, but six months into his marriage, we just had chemistry we couldn't resist. He loved me, but married Melodie because she was more established, but he really loved me. So, he took care of me. He made sure I had a roof over my head and a car and all of my needs met," Jean continued on and on.

By the end of their two-hour conversation, Jean had explained exactly where all of his ATM withdrawals went, indirectly, of course. In fact, after purchasing her a condo and Corvette in cash, along with monthly credit card charges of ten to twenty thousand, it sounded like that accounted for more hidden money than Zach or Ron realized.

Then Jean really dropped a bombshell, unknowingly. "Detective, just because Russ was going through a divorce and was in love with me doesn't mean he killed his wife. He was going through the proper procedures. You know how many couples are having affairs? It doesn't make them murderers. He wasn't even in the country!"

Chapter Twenty

Zach knew Jean really was in the dark. She had no idea about Russ and what he was capable of. He feared for her own safety, being so close to someone so dangerous and callous. But, it was too soon to reveal all of the evidence piling up against Russ. And now he needed to find out about this divorce and let Sean Shafter know that all this money went to Jean's condo, fancy car, fancy shoes and clothes and God knows what else! He also needed to wait to find out the results from the forensics test on the duffel bag found in Russ's hotel room.

Giving Ron additional time to research the missing three million, Zach, Sean and Ron agreed to meet again the following morning. This time they would meet at Zach's office; definitely not Sean's. Ron wasn't going to meet there again until that damn elevator was fixed!

Ron could hardly wait until morning to meet with the team. He had worked dozens of cases where husbands, and sometimes wives, had embezzled money from the marriage. Most of the time, it was simply underreported incomes and having separate savings accounts. But this guy? Jenkins? He was a piece of work! A true master of manipulation. Big money manipulation. The investigation into the whereabouts of the three million borrowed from his children's life insurance policies had revealed massive shenanigans. This clown had bank accounts set up in the Bahamas and Bermuda with over two million in cash deposits (presumably from the ATM withdrawals) and deposits from his commissions earned at Challenge Life. However, the accounts were virtually drained now. And besides the proof of the disbursement instructions from the insurance policies, the three million still had not been found. Nonetheless, Ron had a lot of ammunition to give Shafter and Willis to build their case.

Zach took a few extra moments to clear off a small table in his office, just big enough to seat three people and a bunch of papers. The interrogation rooms were full with other deadbeats being grilled for petty stuff such as breaking and entering and shoplifting. There were no suspected murderers being questioned today. Just on time, Caswell and Shafter showed up, and tagging along was Maltzer. He needed to know how the kids' three million dollars had disappeared.

"Good morning, Mr. Maltzer. I apologize for the tight quarters," Zach said as he reached for a folded chair propped up behind his door. "I hope Ronald has some good news for us today."

Ron began reiterating his findings. He knew that half a million went to Arneson, Jenkins' defense attorney, and a hundred and ten grand went to bail. He told them of the off-shore bank accounts that had been found and that two million dollars worth of deposits went in, via cash deposits and Challenge Life commissions that were diverted into annuities. He further explained that cash withdrawals were made but that there was no record of where the money had gone. He also couldn't find where the three million went, but he certainly was able to show that Russ Jenkins was hiding huge sums of cash from Melodie Jenkins. He also explained to the investigators that the commissions Russ earned from his own children's life insurance policies which were diverted into off-shore annuities also meant that the income wouldn't show up on their taxes for ten to twenty years, so he could further hide the money from Melodie.

"I'm no criminal detective," Ron said, "but it looks like he was planning something for quite some time."

"Listen," Zach continued where Ron left off, "I had a nice long conversation with Jean Cameron yesterday. Remember, she is Russ's Traveling Executive Assistant. Well, it seems she has been assisting him with far more than his work travels for decades. They met in college and were dating up until Russ and Melodie married. He hired Jean at Challenge Life simply so he could lead a double life with her, practically as his second wife." Zach continued to tell the financial team that Russ paid over one million in cash for her condo as well as buying her Corvette with cash. Additionally, she had a credit card in her name where she had unrestricted use, and for which he paid in cash for years. It is believed this is why his off-shore accounts were drained, with no record of purchases.

All of this points to premeditation, but it was still all circumstantial. They needed the smoking gun! About that time, the phone rang. Forensics were done on the duffel bag found in Russ's hotel room the night of the murder. A small speck of blood was found inside the bag and it was tested. The blood belonged to Melodie. It was time to have a meeting with the District Attorney, Mr. Heald over lunch.

Zach explained to the DA the latest developments. He believed it all played out just like this: Russ was dating Melodie and Jean in college and chose Melodie to marry for what appeared to be more stability. However, just after six months of marriage, Russ missed the excitement and sex with Jean and began again with their romantic affair. Originally, Russ had legitimate business to conduct in the Bahamas and in Bermuda. He always stayed at the same hotel and was a regular patron at the Tiki Bar located at his hotel. He met Fillip, the bartender, as well as Sara. When his legitimate business dried up, he fabricated other clients abroad. This gave him the opportunity to hook up with Sara (only when Jean wasn't traveling with him); it gave him the opportunity to travel with Jean as if they were truly a couple; and it gave him the opportunity to continue to have off-shore accounts. As Jean and Russ continued to get even more serious, she began demanding that he leave his wife and make their relationship legitimate. Leaving his wife would be a very expensive option, so rather than that, he hired Jean on at Challenge Life so she could be more a part of his life and avoid getting caught by his wife since she would have even more reasons to be with Russ. He also began taking care of her financially, buying their love nest condo, car, clothes, shoes, and virtually everything she wanted.

Chapter Twenty One

However, Melodie did find out about the affair and immediately began divorce proceedings, using the collaborative model, which was suggested by her divorce attorney.

This meant that they would each retain legal counsel, hire a neutral financial professional and, if needed, one or two psychological coaches, who would provide assistance with the emotional aspects of their marital dissolution. After they retained their attorneys, they hired Sharon Carlisle, CPA. Sharon's job was to collectively examine their income statements and balance sheets, in addition to bank statements (presumably for all of their accounts) over the prior five years. The results of this work would be to provide assistance to the parties and come up with an agreement on finances. Once an agreement was made, then the divorce would be filed. That is why there was no record of divorce at the time of the murder—allowing Russ to lie about the state of their marriage.

Russ knew he was going to lose an enormous amount of money in the event of a divorce, and his hidden accounts might be found. So he believed that he had had no choice but to murder Melodie. He needed to tell Melodie he had a meeting in the Bahamas and when she asked who the client was, he needed to think of a name quickly. He thought of Fillip the bartender and his daughter overheard him tell her he was meeting Philip Moore. He arranged to have the kids stay at their grandparents that fateful night. As Melodie was sleeping, Russ shot her in the head at 4 a.m., changed clothes, putting his blood-splattered clothes and the gun in his duffel bag. He broke the window from the inside, resulting in glass shards falling outside, and disheveled some drawers to make it look like an intruder had been in the home.

He then left for the airport where he met Jean, and together, at 5 a.m. they flew to the Bahamas to meet his imaginary client, using the corporate G4. This allowed him to avoid security checkpoints at a typical airport and to travel from Omaha to the Bahamas in only two plus hours. Russ told Jean they had a meeting at 9 a.m. with their client at the café, but he appeared to stand him up. The client didn't actually stand him up; but simply didn't exist. He used Jean as an alibi so she would also report that Russ was in the Bahamas at the time of the murder. Russ must have disposed of the gun and his bloody clothes somewhere in the Bahamas. They were never found, however, he must have really needed that duffel bag for travels home and despite his efforts to cover his tracks, blood from Melodie transferred into the bag.

When he returned home to the crime scene, he began the performance of his life, appearing as the grieving husband. But it was evident when he checked into the Holiday Inn Express the night of the murder that he must have been a local there, as the clerk simply handed him the room key upon his arrival. This would be odd for a local hotel right down the road from one's own home. He must have had the empty duffel bag packed in his suitcase. He removed it once he got into the room, and either placed it under the bed, or accidentally kicked it under the bed and then later forgot it. He must not have thought it could have possibly had incriminating evidence in it, or he would not have forgotten it. Russ was lucky that Melodie lay unconscious for two hours prior to dying, making his alibi work—at least for six months. Zach disclosed the witness list of those who would be willing to come to court and testify:

Jean ; that Russ and she were having an affair for decades and he has supported her financially for years. She didn't think he killed his wife, but her testimony would be strong.

Beth Jenkins; Russ's daughter would simply state that the client Russ was going to meet was Philip Moore.

Fillip Moore; would testify that he was just a bartender and had no business dealings with Russ outside serving him great drinks.

Ronald Caswell; that Russ had been embezzling millions of dollars from his marriage for six years.

And the medical examiner; that the time of the assault incident differed from the time of death, blowing a hole in Russ's alibi.

"Zach, great work", Mr. Heald congratulated him. "While this case is still circumstantial without the actual gun, I think we can put this arrogant son of a bitch away.

Ronald showed up to the trial wearing his best. His brown slacks were nicely pressed, he wore a brown tweed jacket over his short sleeved buttoned-down blue striped shirt and he even wore a navy blue tie.

"Right on time, Mr. Caswell!" Zach joked. "Well, of course, Mr. W-W-Willis" he joked back as he pointed to his Swiss Chronometer Watch. Another perfect timepiece he had found at an estate sale; this one in Pennsylvania.

The trial lasted for four days. All of the witnesses who promised to testify did so, and they all did well. Fillip seemed to enjoy the limelight and the drama of being the make-believe twenty-two-million-dollar client with whom Russ claimed to have had a scheduled meeting at the time of Melodie's murder. He also disclosed the fling Russ had with Sara when Jean wasn't traveling with him in the Bahamas. Although that was deemed hearsay, everyone believed him, including Jean.

Jean testified to their outlandish affair. She was truthful about the sex and money, but still swore there was no way Russ would kill anyone.

Ron had prepared extensive sets of charts that showed the trace of all funds flowing from Challenge Life commissions into annuities; then more charts showing almost a million dollars in ATM withdrawals, flowing to Jean to support her lifestyle, as well as off shore deposits. He was unable to identify and locate the remaining three million borrowed from his children's accounts. Those funds had never been found.

And the pathologist did explain in detail just how the time of death differed from the time of the shooting, blowing a hole in Russ's alibi.

Kevin Arneson had nothing to go on, with the exception of the fact that they (the prosecution) had no murder weapon. Additionally,

Melodie's blood could have gotten into the duffel bag simply through her own doing. Perhaps she had been at the gym and had used the duffel bag and gotten a cut on her finger, or any other number of ways to explain it.

The jury deliberated for less than three hours. Russ Jenkins was found guilty of first degree murder of his wife and was sentenced to life in prison without the possibility of parole. His narcissism was not halted by the verdict. In fact, he calmly told the jury, the judge, the attorneys, especially his own lawyer, Kevin Arneson, Mr. and Mrs. Farnsworth, and Ashley that these idiots had the wrong man and a dangerous random killer was still on the streets.

Chapter Twenty Two

Jean was devastated. The man she had loved her whole life was a murderer. And, somehow, it would have been a little easier to digest if he had killed his wife to be with her; but no, he had killed his wife over money. It could have just as easily been Jean he'd killed if she had married him first. She couldn't grasp how any man could love no one but himself. How could a successful man who had everything going for him and four lovely children, one of whom needed special care, take the life of the very person who was the nucleus of their being? She realized she never ever really knew who Russ Jenkins was— until now. She quickly scribbled a note to give to him. As Russ was led out of the courtroom in handcuffs, she slipped it into his pocket. He smiled at her and simply said, "I love you, too".

D.A. Heald, Zach Willis, Ronald Caswell and Sean Shafter all hit the local pub to celebrate justice for Melodie with the biggest, coldest beer they had. This was a routine Zach lived by. Every time, when a conviction was granted, he celebrated justice for the victim. Not only in honor of the victim, but also in honor of his own kids being protected. For every conviction, his own kids were that much safer.

It still bothered Zach Willis that neither the three million dollars nor the murder weapon had ever been located. This would forever haunt him!

"Mr. Caswell", Zach reached out his right hand, "this had better not be the last I see of you. You're damn good at what you do and I just might need you again."

"You just call me anytime, Detective Willis. Will you pay me more than this guy, Shafter pays me?" "Oh, come on, now, Ron. Is it that bad?" Sean responded with another toast.

Their toast was interrupted by Zach's phone. "Yes, Willis here."

"Detective Willis, this is Captain Brooks, Chief of Homicide at Boston P D. Your reputation precedes you. Congratulations on the Jenkins conviction today. We need a guy like you here in Boston. Can we talk?"

EPILOGUE

PART I – OMAHA is the first of five sections comprising *Dying To Divorce.*

PARTS II and III begin when Zach Willis moves to Boston with his family to enhance his career. In the next four cases, Zach has an opportunity to solve some unusual mysteries in his new role as lead homicide detective for Boston P.D.

These next sections will include:

- "Cold Case"

- "Basic Black & Pearls"

- "There Goes The Judge"

- "The Bridge"

CPSIA information can be obtained
at www.ICGtesting.com
Printed in the USA
FFOW05n2011161016

9 780692 785256